Pr   i

A   i

1	**Ins... ....**	**1**
	Why Windows NT?	1
	The Prism project	3
	Multitasking	3
	Resource protection	11
	Multi-threaded software	12
	32 bit processing and addressing	14
	Advantages for the user	18
2	**Installing Windows NT**	**21**
	CD-ROM or floppy	21
	Before installation	21
	The installation commands	24
	The installation procedure itself	25
	Booting Windows NT	26
	The system check	28
	After installation	29
	Installation variations	29
3	**The Windows '95 shell**	**30**
	The Windows '95 desktop	31
	Window handling	*32*
	The window menu	*33*
	The Taskbar	34
	Copying and moving files	35
	The left mouse button	*35*
	The right mouse button	*35*
	Shortcuts	36
	The Recycle Bin	36
	The Windows NT Explorer	37
	The Programs menu	*37*
	The Documents menu	*38*
	The settings options	*38*
	Find\\All Files	*39*
	Find\\Computer	*41*
	Run	*41*
	Shutdown	*41*
	The Control Panel	42
	Common window menus	42
	The File menu	*43*

The Edit menu	43
The View menu	44
The Explore command	48
The Tools menu	48
Taskbar configuration	49
Start Menu Programs	49
Taskbar options	51
My computer	52
Properties	54
Network Neighborhood	56
Other right hand button tricks	57
Clicking on the desktop	57
4 Accessories	**59**
Calculator	59
The Edit menu	60
The View menu	60
The Help menu	60
Clock	60
The Settings menu	61
Cardfile	61
The File menu	61
The Edit menu	62
The View menu	63
The Card menu	63
The Search Menu	64
The Help menu	64
Notepad	64
The File menu	65
The Edit menu	65
The Search menu	65
The Help menu	65
Paint	66
The File menu	67
The Edit menu	67
The View menu	68
The Image menu	69
The Options menu	70
The Help menu	70
Chat	70
HyperTerminal	70
Installing a modem	73
Creating a connection	74
Changing a connection	76
The File menu	82
The Edit menu	83
The View menu	83
The Call menu	84

Newnes
Windows NT
Pocket Book

By the same author

Microprocessor Architectures: RISC, CISC and DSP

Newnes MAC User's Pocket Book

Newnes UNIX™ Pocket Book

Effective PC Networking

VMEbus: a practical companion

PowerPC: a practical companion

The PC and MAC handbook: systems, upgrades and troubleshooting

Newnes PowerPC Programming Pocket Book

The Multimedia and Communications Handbook

In preparation

Essential Linux

Migrating to Windows NT

All books published by Butterworth-Heinemann

About the author:

Through his work with Motorola Semiconductors, the author has been involved in the design and development of microprocessor based systems since 1982. These designs have included VMEbus systems, microcontrollers, IBM PCs, Apple Macintoshes, and both CISC and RISC based multi-processor systems, while using operating systems as varied as MS-DOS, UNIX, Macintosh OS and real time kernels.

An avid user of computer systems, he has had over 60 articles and papers published in the electronics press as well as several books.

Newnes
Windows NT
Pocket Book

Second edition

Steve Heath

Newnes
An imprint of Butterworth-Heinemann

Newnes

An imprint of Butterworth-Heinemann
Linacre House, Jordan Hill, Oxford OX2 8DP
A division of Reed Educational and
Professional Publishing Ltd

$\mathcal{R}$ A member of the Reed Elsevier plc group

OXFORD   BOSTON   JOHANNESBURG
MELBOURNE   NEW DELHI   SINGAPORE

First published 1996
Second edition 1997

© Steve Heath 1996, 1997

British Library Cataloguing in Publication Data
A catalogue record for this book is available
from the British Library

ISBN 0 7506 3422 7

Library of Congress Cataloguing in Publication Data
A catalogue record for this book is available
from the Library of Congress

Typeset by *Steve Heath*

Printed and bound in Great Britain at The Bath Press, Bath

The Transfer menu	*85*
The Help menu	*86*
The right hand button	*86*
Sound recorder	87
The File menu	*87*
The Edit menu	*87*
The Effects menu	*88*
The Help menu	*88*
Volume control	88
Character map	89
CD Player	90
The Disc menu	*90*
The View menu	*90*
The Options menu	*91*
The Help menu	*91*
Media player	91
The File menu	*92*
The Edit menu	*92*
The Device menu	*92*
The Scale menu	*92*
The Help menu	*92*
WordPad	93
The File menu	*94*
The Edit menu	*94*
The View menu	*95*
The Insert menu	96
The Format menu	96
The Help menu	*99*
The right hand button	99
Telnet	99
Dial-up networking	99
Phone Dialler	*100*
Imaging	101
Clipbook viewer	101
Object Packager	101
5 The Explorer	**103**
The Explorer window	103
The Explorer menus	104
The File menu	*104*
The Edit menu	*105*
The View menu	*106*
The Help menu	*109*

6	**Networking**	**111**
	Windows NT workstations and servers	111
	Domains, workgroups, computers and users	111
	Installing Windows NT, Windows '95 and WFW3.11 support	113
	Installing the hardware	*113*
	Initial software installation with the wizard	*113*
	Normal installation	119
	Identification sub-panel	*119*
	Adapters sub-panel	*120*
	Protocols sub-panel	*123*
	Services sub-panel	*125*
	Bindings sub-panel	*126*
	Connecting to another computer	127
	Using the Network Neighborhood	*127*
	Using the Windows NT Explorer	*127*
	Connecting to network disk drives	*127*
	Disconnecting from network drives	*128*
	Making files and folders shareable	*129*
	Multiple shares to the same resource	*135*
	Recognising shared resources	*135*
	Stopping sharing	*135*
	Multiple permissions	136
	Installing AppleTalk support	136
7	**Control panels**	**140**
	Accessibility options	141
	Add/remove Program Properties	143
	Console Window Properties	145
	Fonts	147
	Ports	148
	Internet	150
	Mouse	151
	Keyboard	153
	Printers	156
	Regional	156
	SCSI Adapters	157
	System	158
	Recovery	*160*
	Virtual memory	*161*
	Tasking	*162*
	Hardware profiles	*162*
	User profiles	*162*
	Telephony	163
	Tape Devices	165

Date and Time 166
Display settings 167
Server 171
Sound 172
Network settings 172
Devices 172
Services 173
UPS 173
Multimedia 174

8   Printing   180
Concepts 180
The Printers control panel window 180
Installing a printer 182
Selecting a port 182
Connecting to an AppleTalk printer 183
Defining the printer type 185
Installing multiple printers 187
Configuring a printer 188
Controlling a printer 194
The File menu 194
The Edit menu 195
The View menu 196
The Help menu 198
Controlling a printer queue 198
The Printer menu 198
The Document menu 199
The View menu 200
The Help menu 200
Summary 200

9   Administrative tools   201
The User Manager 201
The User menu 202
The Policies menu 206
The Options menu 209
Disk Administrator 209
The Partition menu 210
The Tools menu 213
The Options menu 215
Event Viewer 216
The Log menu 217
The View menu 218
The Options menu 219
Performance Monitor 219
The File menu 219

      The Edit menu   *220*
      The View menu   *221*
      The Options menu   *222*
   Backup   223
      Installing a tape drive   *223*
      The Backup main window   *224*
      Selecting files   *225*
      The Operations menu   *225*
      The Tree menu   *226*
      The View menu   *227*
      The Select menu   *228*
      The Window Menu   *228*
   Windows NT Diagnostics   228
      Version   *228*
      System   *229*
      Memory   *230*
      Services   *230*
      Display   *232*
      Drives   *233*
      Resources   *234*
      Environment   *235*
      Network   *235*
   Remote Access Admin   236
      The Server menu   *236*
      The Users menu   *237*
      The Options menu   *237*

10   **How do I do that?**   **238**
   Changing the system   238
      Changing the desktop   *238*
      Changing the video   *238*
      Changing the environmental variables   *238*
      Changing the boot up procedure   *238*
      Changing the date and time formats   *238*
      Changing the keyboard layout   *238*
      Changing the mouse settings   *238*
      Changing the sound settings   *239*
      Changing the disk configurations   *239*
      Adding/removing tape drives   *239*
      Adding/removing SCSI drives
      and CD-ROMs   *239*
   Files and directories   239
      Copying   *239*
      Deleting   *239*
      Renaming   *240*
      Moving   *240*
      Backing up   *240*
      Finding   *240*
      Adding more disk space   *240*

Keyboard alternatives 241
Moving to different buttons 241
Using the keyboard instead of a mouse 241
Navigating the screen 241
Selecting other applications 241
Deleting other tasks 242
Minimise and maximise windows 242
Adjusting windows 242
Creating a program group or item 243
Deleting a program group 243
Deleting a program item 243
Networks 244
Connecting to a network drive 244
Disconnecting a network drive 244
Connecting to a network printer 244
Disconnecting a network printer 244
*Adding/removing network boards
and drivers* 244
Passwords 244
Changing 244
Forgotten 244
Locked out accounts 244
Screen savers 245
Printing 245
Creating a printer 245
Accessing a printer on another system 245
Assigning the default printer 245
Using a different printer 245
Deleting documents 245
Pausing a printer 245
Resuming a paused printer 246
Pausing a document 246
Resuming a document 246
Setting up the printer 246
Page sizes 246
Screen dumps 246

Appendices

A   **Hayes compatible
modem commands** 247

B   **How do I do that with
Windows NT 3.x?** 258

Index 267

Preface

For many, Windows NT is an operating system only for servers and high powered network systems and not meant for use in PCs and RISC based workstations. The main reason for this is the hardware that is needed to run it successfully compared with Windows 3.11. With the advent of Windows '95, and its demand for more memory and processing power, the hardware difference is less and therefore, there is a growing interest in using Windows NT as the Windows environment instead of Windows 3.11 or Windows '95. This advantage is even greater with the advent of the Windows NT version 4 with its Windows '95 shell which provides the Windows '95 environment with all the advantages of Windows NT. This, coupled with the message from Microsoft that Windows NT is the basis of all its future desktop operating systems, and it is not surprising that it has gained so much interest. For environments where connectivity, security and stability are essential, Windows NT provides an ideal solution .

Windows NT is especially suited for users that have come from UNIX backgrounds and expect levels of security, stability and functionality which neither Windows 3.11 or Windows '95 can offer. It must be said that Windows '95 relies a lot on the developments and technology that came with Windows NT to provide its new functions. This is a trend that will undoubtedly continue with Windows and Windows NT becoming a single environment at some point in the future. In this respect, Windows NT is the future of the Windows environment.

This book is a concise guide to using the Windows NT operating system and covers its internals and how it differs from Windows and Windows '95, its installation and use. The method used is to group like utilities together so that accessories are handled in one chapter, the administration tools in another and so on. To provide a broader scope, the last chapter covers the main frequently performed tasks and gives simple answers and pointers on how to perform them. For completeness and to provide support for the previous version 4.0, an appendix has been included that describes the old shell that uses the Windows 3.1 interface.

The material is based on Windows NT version 4.0 with its Windows '95 shell, running on both Intel PC and PowerPC based systems.

I have used the following nomenclature to indicate options within menus: **File\\Exit** indicates that the Exit command from the File menu is referred to. In addition, underlined letters in command names indicate the keyboard shortcut for that command. With the **E_x_it** command, typing x will activate it with the menu available on the screen.

I would like to express my thanks to Motorola for their encouragement and help and once again, to Sue Carter for her support and editing skills.

Steve Heath

Acknowledgements

By the nature of this book, many hardware and software products are identified by their trade marks or trade names. In these cases, these designations are claimed as legally protected trademarks by the companies that make these products. It is not the author's or the publisher's intention to use these names generically, and the reader is cautioned to investigate a trademark before using it as a generic term, rather than a reference to a specific product to which it is attached.

All trademarks are acknowledged, in particular:

- IBM, IBM PC, PC XT, PowerPC, PC AT and PC-DOS are trademarks of International Business Machines.

- Windows, Windows '95, MS-DOS, Windows NT, Windows for Workgroups are all trademarks of Microsoft.

While the information in this book has been carefully checked for accuracy, neither author nor publisher assume any responsibility or liability for its use or any results, or any infringement of patents or other rights of third parties that would result.

As technical characteristics are subject to rapid change, the information contained is presented for guidance and education only. For exact detail and design, always consult the manufacturers' data and specifications.

Many of the techniques within this book can destroy data and such techniques must be used with extreme caution. Again, neither author nor publisher assume any responsibility or liability for their use or any results.

1   Inside Windows NT

Windows NT has been portrayed as many different things during its short lifetime. When it first appeared, it was perceived by many as the replacement for Windows 3.1, an alternative to UNIX and finally has settled down as operating system for workstations, servers and power users. This chameleon like change was not due to any real changes in the product but were caused by a mixture of aspirations and misunderstandings.

Windows NT will eventually replace Windows 3.1 and Windows '95 and parts of the its technology have already found themselves incorporated into Windows '95 and Windows for Workgroups. Whether the replacement is through a merging of the operating system technologies or through a sharing of common technology, only time will tell. The important message is that the Windows NT environment is becoming prevalent, especially with Microsoft's aim of a single set of programming interfaces that will allow an application to run on any of its operating system environments.

Why Windows NT?

The question that must people ask when contemplating using Windows NT, is what does it offer over Windows 3.1 or even Windows '95. This section provides the common answers to this question.

- Portability

  Most PC based operating systems were written in low-level assembler language instead of a high level language such as C or C++. This decision was taken to provide smaller programs sizes and the best possible performance. The disadvantage is that the operating system and applications are now dependent on the hardware platform and is extremely difficult to move from platform to another. MS-DOS is written in 8086 assembler which is incompatible with the M68000 processors used in the Apple Macintosh. For a software company like Microsoft, this has an additional threat of being dependent on a single processor platform. If the platform changes — who remembers the Z80 and 6502 processors which were the mainstays of the early PCs — then its software technology becomes obsolete.

  With an operating system that is written in a high level language and is portable to other platforms, it allows Microsoft and other application developers to be less hardware dependent.

- True multitasking

  While more performant operating systems such as UNIX and VMS offer the ability to run multiple applicatic~ simultaneously, this facility is not really available the Windows and MS-DOS environments (a full explanation of what they can do and the difference will be offered later in the chapter). This is now becoming a very important aspect for both users and developers alike so that the full performance of today's processors can be utilised.

- Multi-threaded

Multi-threading refers to a way of creating software that can be re-used without having to have multiple copies of the code or memory spaces. This leads to more efficient use of both memory and code.

- Processor independent

Unlike Windows and MS-DOS which are completely linked to the Intel 80x86 architecture, Windows NT through its portability is processor independent and has been ported to other processor architectures such as Motorola's PowerPC, DEC's Alpha architecture and MIPS RISC processor systems.

- Multiprocessor support

Windows NT uses a special interface to the processor hardware which makes it independent of the processor architecture that it is running on. As a result, this not only gives processor independence but also allows the operating system to run on multiprocessor systems.

- Security and POSIX support

Windows NT offers several levels of security through is use of a multi-part access token. This token is created and verified when a user logs onto the system and contains IDs for the user, the group he is assigned to, privileges and other information. In addition, an audit trail is also provided to allow an administrator to check who has used the system, when they used it and what they did. While an overkill for a single user, this is invaluable with a system that is either used by many or connected to a network.

The POSIX standard defines a set of interfaces that allow POSIX compliant applications to easily be ported between POSIX compliant computer systems.

Both security and POSIX support are commercially essential to satisfy purchasing requirements from government departments, both in the US and the rest of the world.

- Networking support

Windows NT is available in two forms: the server version which as its name suggest turns a PC or workstation platform into a network server and the workstation version which can act as a network client to the server and access its files. The nomenclature is not quite as clean as it could be because Windows NT Workstation is capable of acting as a server in peer-to-peer networks where all the workstations are connected together on the network and allow each other to share files and printers.

The networking protocols supported cover virtually the whole range of commercially available products and include TCP/IP, LAN Manager as used with Windows for Workgroups, Netware and so on.

- MS-DOS and Windows 3.x compatibility

  Last but not least, it can provide MS-DOS, Windows 3.1 and Windows '95 environments and run existing MS-DOS and Windows applications even on non-Intel processors through the use of emulation techniques.

The Prism project

The Windows NT development came about through DEC's decision not to proceed with its successor to the VMS operating system called Prism. Prism had been under development for three years and its cancellation came as a shock to everyone concerned. The project director, David Cutler subsequently left DEC shortly after the cancellation and joined Microsoft in 1988 to start work on what was going to be come Windows NT.

Windows NT encompasses many of the ideas and concepts that would have gone into Prism if it had been allowed to continue. Through this strange quirk of fate, Microsoft were able to harness Cutler and most of his team and also exploit their knowledge of how to design operating systems.

Multitasking

Multitasking is the ability to run multiple pieces of software simultaneously on the same computer. This technique is not new to the computer world but it is relatively new to the PC. Although the ability to multitask — to run multiple applications at the same time is provided by Windows 3.1 for example, its implementation is not true multitasking and has several limitations when compared to the multitasking offered by a UNIX system. Windows NT offers true multitasking and is one of the major differences between it and Windows 3.1. To fully understand its implications, consider the different levels of multitasking that have been implemented within the operating system predecessors of Windows NT.

Singletasking — MS-DOS

Most operating systems used on PCs today, such as MS-DOS, can only execute one application at a time. This means that only one user can use the computer at any time, with the further limitation that only one application can run at a time. While a spreadsheet is executing, the PC can only wait for commands and data from the keyboard. This is a great waste of computer power because the PC could be executing other programs or applications or, alternately, allow other users to run their software on it.

To try and provide this support, many TSR(terminate and stay resident) type programs were written for MS-DOS which gives a certain level of multitasking, albeit under manual control. These programs load themselves into memory and adjust the memory parameters so that MS-DOS believes that the memory that they have taken is not present. This ensures that any subsequent MS-DOS programs will not overwrite these memory areas and destroy the program(s) that are resident there. The technique for doing this is built into the TSR. When it executes, it loads itself, adjusts the memory parameters and attaches itself to an external event such as a pressing a particular key sequence. Once completed, it terminates its execution, leaving its main program in memory.

Using TSRs gives the impression that the user is multitasking and in some ways this is a true statement but it is not completely the case. While the TSRs are resident in memory, they will not execute until explicitly told to in response to an event. If no event happens e.g. the designated key sequence is not pressed, the program will not execute. In addition, TSRs are special programs that are different from a normal application such as WordStar or ProComm.

Multitasking — UNIX

A multi-tasking operating system such as UNIX works by dividing the computer processor's time into multiple discrete time slots. Each task or application requires a certain number of time slots to complete its execution. The operating system kernel decides automatically which process can have the next slot, so instead of an application executing continuously until completion, its execution is interleaved with other applications and tasks. This sharing of processor time between applications and tasks gives the user the illusion that he is the only one using the system.

Such operating systems are based around a multi-tasking kernel which controls the time slicing mechanisms. A time slice is the time period each process has for execution before it is stopped and replaced during a context switch. This is periodically triggered by a hardware interrupt from the system timer. This interrupt may also provide the system clock and several interrupts may be executed and counted before a context switch is performed.

When a context switch is performed, as shown , the current process is interrupted, the processor's registers are saved in a special table for that particular process, and it is placed back on the 'ready' list to await another time slice. Special tables, often called control blocks, store all the information the system requires about the process, for example, its memory usage, its priority level within the system and its error handling. It is this context information that is switched when one process is replaced by another.

Time slice

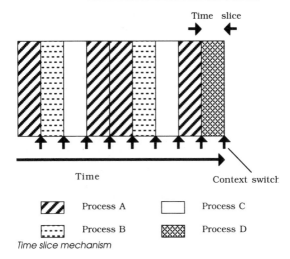

Time

Context switch

	Process A		Process C

Time slice mechanism

The 'ready' list contains all the processes and their status and is used by the scheduler to decide which process is allocated the next time slice. The scheduling algorithm determines the sequence and takes into account a process's priority and present status. If a process is waiting for an I/O call to complete, it will be held in limbo until the call is complete.

Once a process is selected, the processor registers and status at the time of its last context switch are loaded back and the processor is started. The new process carries on as if nothing had happened, until the next context switch takes place. This is the basic method behind all multi-tasking operating systems, including UNIX, DEC's VMS and Windows NT. One important characteristic to understand is that the computer system cannot magically maintain the same computation and processing throughput if additional users and processes are added to its workload. As the system is loaded, response times to commands depend on how much time the scheduler within the kernel can allocate to each application. If the system is lightly loaded, it may appear that the system has an instantaneous reaction. This is caused by the system devoting all it processing power to perform a single request. As the system becomes loaded, this amount of time decreases and the same amount of work will take longer because it is regularly interrupted by other processes.

Co-operative multitasking — Windows 3.1

With Windows 3.1, multitasking is provided using a different mechanism. Instead of dividing the processing time into slots as previously described and allocating a slot to each application, a single time slot is allocated to applications and the applications themselves actually co-operate amongst themselves and allow others to have a share in processing. If there is a word processor

and spreadsheet running, the word processor in the foreground —
i.e. its window is active and it is the application that the user is
currently using — will give up some of its processing time to the
spreadsheet and the spreadsheet will be able to continue processing in the background. The effect for the user is the appearance of
multitasking but it is heavily dependent on the applications
discipline to co-operate. This technique is described as co-opera-
tive multitasking because it gives the illusion of multitasking but
requires the applications rather than the operating system itself to
decide who runs when.

This scheme is reasonable but does suffer from several flaws:
it relies totally on the co-operation of all the applications and this
can be a major problem when running older MS-DOS software
which was never written to work in such an environment. It is
possible and frequently occurs that an un-cooperative application
completely hogs all the processing time and prevents any other
application from running. The effect can range from the mildly
annoying to the extremely frustrating depending on what the other
applications need to do. If data is being transferred in the background, then this may stop and the data lost or corrupted.

Pre-emptive multitasking

The multi-tasking environment used within Windows 3.1 and
3.11 is a form of multi-tasking but involves the application's co-
operation in providing the ability to run multiple applications
simultaneously. An alternative way of designing a multi-tasking
environment is to remove the application's involvement and let
the operating system control and provide the multi-tasking environment itself. In this case, the operating system will allocate
processing time to an application depending an algorithm that
determines its characteristics. Typically, the algorithms use a
form of priority to determine which application should run next.

The time slice algorithm described previously is fine for
many environments but does have some interesting drawbacks. A
high priority task can hog all the processing time and thus cause
all the other applications to remain in limbo. It also infers that a
higher priority application can only take over the processing
either when the currently executing application relinquishes control at a convenient point — e.g. its made a system request and is
waiting for the operating system to complete it — or when its time
slice is complete. As a result, any event within the system that
needs an application or task to process it may have to wait until the
current time slice has completed before it can execute. With many
events that are not time critical, this may not be a problem,
however this is not always the case and the potential delay can
cause a real difficulty.

Many multitasking operating systems available today are
described as "real-time". These operating systems provide additional facilities allowing applications that would normally interface directly with the microprocessor architecture to use interrupts and drive peripherals to do so without the operating system
blocking such activities. Many multitasking operating systems

prevent the user from accessing such sensitive resources. This overzealous caring can prevent many operating systems from being used in applications such as industrial control.

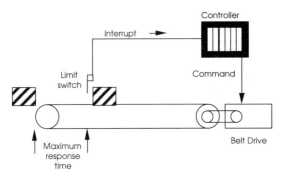

Example of a real time response

A characteristic of a real-time operating system is its defined response time to external stimuli. If a peripheral generates an interrupt, a real-time system will acknowledge and start to service it within a maximum defined time. Such response times vary from system to system, but the maximum time specified is a worst case figure, and will not be exceeded due to changes in factors such as system workload.

Any system meeting this requirement can be described as real-time, irrespective of the actual value, but typical industry accepted figures for context switches and interrupt response times are about 100 microseconds.

The consequences to industrial control of not having a real-time characteristic can be disastrous. If a system is controlling an automatic assembly line, and does not respond in time to a request from a conveyor belt limit switch to stop the belt, the results are easy to imagine. The response does not need to be instantaneous — if the limit switch is set so that there are three seconds to stop the belt, any system with a guaranteed worst case response of less than three seconds can meet this real-time requirement.

For an operating system to be real-time, its internal mechanisms need to show real-time characteristics so that the internal processes sequentially respond to external interrupts in guaranteed times.

When an interrupt is generated, the current process is interrupted to allow the kernel to acknowledge the interrupt and obtain the vector number that it needs to determine how to handle it. A typical technique is to use the kernel's interrupt handler to update a linked list which contains information on all the processes that need to be notified of the interrupt.

To be practical, a real-time operating system has to guarantee maximum response times for its interrupt handler, event passing mechanisms, scheduler algorithm and provide system calls to allow tasks to attach and handle interrupts.

With the conveyor belt example above, a typical software configuration would dedicate a task to controlling the conveyor belt. This task would make several system calls on start-up to access the parallel I/O peripheral that interfaces the system to components such as the drive motors and limit switches and tells the kernel that certain interrupt vectors are attached to the task and are handled by its own interrupt handling routine.

Once the task has set everything up, it remains dormant until an event is sent by other tasks to switch the belt on or off. If a limit switch is triggered, it sets off an interrupt which forces the kernel to handle it. The currently executing task stops, the kernel handler searches the task interrupt attachment linked list, and places the controller task on the ready list, with its own handler ready to execute. At the its appropriate time slice, the handler runs, accesses the peripheral and switches off the belt. This result may not be normal, and so the task also sends event messages to the others, informing them that it has acted independently and may force other actions. Once this has been done, the task goes back to its dormant state awaiting further commands.

Real-time operating systems have other advantages: to prevent a system from power failure usually needs a guaranteed response time so that the short time between the recognition of and the actual power failure can be used to store vital data and bring the system down in a controlled manner. Many operating systems actually have a power fail module built into the kernel so that no time is lost in executing the module code.

A pre-emptive multitasking system solves the problem by allowing a higher priority application or task to stop the current executing application and take over the processing. This pre-emption of the current application and its replacement provides a faster and guaranteed context switch time which can be several orders of magnitude shorter than the time slice period — typically microseconds instead of milliseconds.

To ensure that the correct applications run at the right time, priorities are assigned to the applications and tasks within the system so that higher priority applications and tasks will lock out lower priority ones. By selecting the appropriate priorities to the applications — high priority to time critical operations and lower priority to the non-time critical ones — the system performance can be tuned between a range of characteristics.

This discussion of conveyor belts and power fail modules may seem a far cry from a desktop PC operating system, but many of the problems faced by the conveyor belt are present within a high performance desktop PC connected within a network. The PC must be able to multitask and will frequently need to handle and transfer data coming from a network, the PC's peripherals and so on. If this data is not processed with a given time, the data will either be lost or performance will be sacrificed. This is no different from the real time constraint imposed on the conveyor belt system. Even the need to recognise external power failures is there with the support of uninterruptable power supplies!

Windows NT characteristics

Windows NT is a pre-emptive multi-tasking environment that will run multiple applications simultaneously and uses a priority based mechanism to determine the running order. It is capable of providing real time support in that it has a priority mechanism and fast response times for interrupts and so on, but it is less deterministic — there is a wider range of response times — when compared to a real time operating system such as pSOS or OS-9 used in industrial applications. It can be suitable for many real time applications with less critical timing characteristics and this is a big advantage over the Windows 3.1 and Windows '95 environments.

Process priorities

Windows NT calls all applications, device drivers, software tasks and so on processes and this nomenclature will be used from now on. Each process can be assigned one of 32 priority levels which determines its scheduling priority.

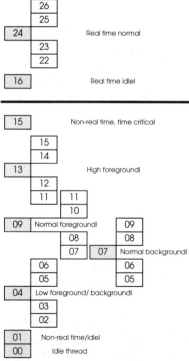

Windows NT priority levels — base class levels are shaded

The 32 levels are divided into two groups called the real-time and dynamic classes. The real time classes comprise priority levels 16 through to 31 and the dynamic classes use priority levels 15 to 0. Within these two groups, certain priorities are defined as base classes and processes are allocated a base process. Independent parts of a process — these are called threads — can be assigned their own priority level which are derived from the base class priority and can be ±2 levels different. In addition, a process cannot move from a real-time class to a dynamic one.

The diagram shows how the base classes are organised. The first point is that within a given dynamic base class, it is possible for a lot of overlap. Although a process may have a lower base class compared to another process, it may be at a higher priority than the other one depending on the actual priority level that has been assigned to it. The real-time class is a little simpler although again there is some possibility for overlap.

User applications like word processors, spread sheets and so on run in the dynamic class and their priority will change depending on the application status. Bring an application from the background to the foreground by expanding the shrunk icon or by switching to that application will change its priority appropriately so that it gets allocated a higher priority and therefore more processing. Real time processes include device drivers handling the keyboard, cursor, file system and other similar activities.

Interrupt priorities

The concept of priorities is not solely restricted to the pre-emption priority previously described. Those priorities come into play when an event or series of events occur. The events themselves are also controlled by 32 priority levels defined by the hardware abstraction layer (HAL).

31	Hardware error interrupt
30	Powerfail interrupt
29	Inter-processor interrupt
28	Clock interrupt
27-12	Standard IBM PC AT interrupt levels 0 to 15
11-4	Reserved(not generally used)
3	Software debugger
2-0	Software interrupts for device drivers etc.

Interrupt priorities

The interrupt priorities work in a similar way to those found on a microprocessor: if an interrupt of a higher priority than the current interrupt priority mask is generated, the current processing will stop and be replaced by the associated routines for the new higher priority level. In addition, the mask will be raised to match that of the higher priority. When the higher priority processing has been completed, the previous processing will be restored and allowed to continue. The interrupt priority mask will also be restored to its previous value.

Within Windows NT, the interrupt processing is also subject to the multi-tasking priority levels as well. Depending on how these are assigned to the interrupt priority levels, the processing of a high priority interrupt may be delayed until a higher priority process has completed. It makes sense therefore to have high priority interrupts processed by processes with high priority scheduling levels. Comparing the interrupts and the priority levels shows that this maxim has been followed. Software interrupts used to communicate between processes are allocated both low interrupt and scheduling priorities. Time critical interrupts such as the clock and inter-processor interrupts are handled as real time processes and are allocated the higher real time scheduling priorities.

The combination of both priority schemes provide a fairly complex and flexible method of structuring how an external and internal events and messages are handled.

Resource protection

If a system is going to run multiple applications simultaneously then it must be able to ensure that one application doesn't affect another. This is done through several layers of resource protection. Resource protection within MS-DOS and Windows 3.1 is a rather hit and miss affair. There is nothing to stop an application from directly accessing an I/O port or other physical device and if it did so, it could potentially interfere with another application that was already using it. Although the Windows 3.1 environment can provide some resource protection, it is of collaboration level and not mandatory. It is without doubt a case of self-regulation as opposed to obeying the rules of the system.

Protecting memory

The most important resource to protect is memory. Each process is allocated its own memory which is protected from interference by other processes through programming the memory management unit. This part of the processor's hardware tracks the executing process and ensures that any access to memory that it has not been allocated or given permission to use is stopped.

Protecting hardware

Hardware such as I/O devices are also protected by the memory management unit and any direct access is prevented. Such accesses have to be made through a device driver and in this way the device driver can control who has access to a serial port and so on. A mechanism called a spinlock is also used to control access. A process can only access a device or port if associated spinlock is not set. If it is someone else is using it and the process must wait until they have finished using it.

Coping with crashes

If a process crashes then it is important for the operating system to maintain as much of the system as possible. This requires that the operating system as well as other applications must have its own memory and resources given to it. To ensure this is the case, processes that are specific to user applications are run in a user mode while operating system processes are executed in a special kernel mode. These modes are kept separate from each other and are protected. In addition, the operating system has to have detailed knowledge of the resources used by the crashed process so that it can clean up the process, remove it and thus free up the resources that it used. In some special cases, such as power failures where the operating system may have a limited amount of time to shut down the system in a controlled manner or save as much of the system data as it can, resources are dedicated specifically for this functionality. For example, the second highest interrupt priority is allocated to signalling a power failure.

Windows NT is very resilient to system crashes and while processes can crash, the system will continue. This is essentially due to the use of user and kernel modes coupled with extensive resource protection. Compared to Windows 3.1 and MS-DOS, this resilience is a big advantage.

Multi-threaded software

There is a third difference with Windows NT that many other operating system do not provide in that it supports multithreaded processes.

Processes can support several independent processing paths or threads. A process may consist of several independent sections and thus form several different threads in that the context of the processing in one thread may be different from that in another thread. In other words, the process has all the resources defined that it will use and if the process can support multi-threaded operations, the scheduler will see multiple threads going through the process. A good analogy is a production line. If the production line is single threaded, it can only produce a single end product at a time. If it is multithreaded, it separates the production process into several independent parts and each part can work on a different product. As soon as the first operation has taken place, a second thread can be started. The threads do not have to follow the same path and can vary their route through the process.

The diagram shows a simple multi-threaded operation with each thread being depicted by a different shading. As the first thread progresses through, a second thread can be started. As that progresses through, a third can commence and so on. The resources required to process the multiple threads in this case are the same as if only one thread was supported.

The advantage of multi-threaded operation is that the process does not have to be duplicated every time it is used: a new thread can be started. The disadvantage is that the process programming must ensure that there is no contention or conflict between the various threads that it supports. All the threads that exist in the process can access each other's data structures and even files. The operating system who normally polices the environment is powerless in this case. Threads within Windows NT derive their priority from that of the process although the level can be adjusted within a limited range.

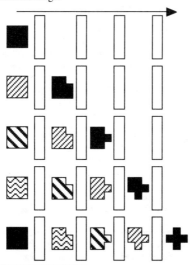

A multi-threaded operation

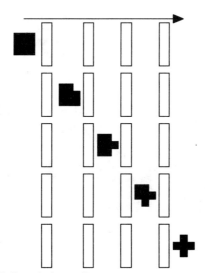

A single-threaded operation

32 bit processing and addressing

Addressing space

The addressing space within Windows NT is radically different from that experienced within MS-DOS and Windows 3.1. It provides a 4 Gbyte virtual address space for each process which is linearly addressed using 32 bit address values. This is different from the segmented memory map that MS-DOS and Windows have to use. A segmented memory scheme uses 16 bit addresses to provide address spaces of only 64 Kbytes. If addresses beyond this space have to be used, special support is needed to change the segment address to point to a new segment. Gone are the different types of memory such as extended and expanded.

This change towards a large 32 bit linear address space improves the environment for software applications and increases their performance and capabilities to handle large data structures. The operating system library that the applications use is called WIN32 to differentiate it from the WIN16 libraries that Windows 3.1 applications use. Applications that use the WIN32 library are known as 32 bit or even native — this term is also used for Windows NT applications that use the same instruction set as the host processor and therefore do not need to emulate a different architecture.

To provide support for legacy MS-DOS and Windows 3.1 applications, Windows NT has a 16 bit environment which simulates the segmented architecture that these application use.

Virtual memory

The idea behind virtual memory is to provide more memory than physically present within the system. To make up the shortfall, a file or files are used to provide overflow storage for applications which are to big to fit in the system RAM at one time. Such applications memory requirements are divided into pages and unused pages are stored on disk.

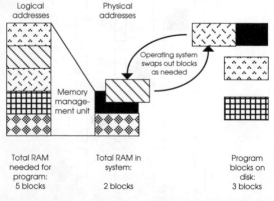

Logical addresses   Physical addresses

Operating system swaps out blocks as needed

Memory management unit

Total RAM needed for program: 5 blocks

Total RAM in system: 2 blocks

Program blocks on disk: 3 blocks

A virtual memory scheme

When the processor wishes to access a page which is not resident in memory, the memory management hardware asserts a page fault, selects the least used page in memory and swaps it with the wanted page stored on disk. Therefore, to reduce the system overhead, fast mass storage and large amounts of RAM are normally required.

Windows NT uses a swap file to provide a virtual memory environment. The file is dynamic in size and varies with the amount of memory that all the software including the operating system, device driver, and applications require. The Windows 3.1 swap file is limited to about 30 Mbytes in size and this effectively limits the amount of virtual memory that it can support.

The internal architecture

The internal architecture is shown in the diagram and depicts the components that run in the user and kernel modes. Most of the operating system runs in the kernel mode with the exception of the security and WIN32 subsystems.

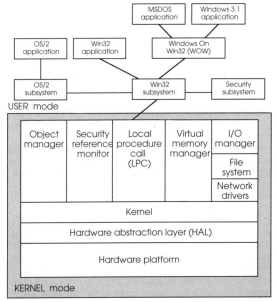

The internal Windows NT architecture

MS-DOS, Windows 3.1 and OS/2 support

Windows NT can run OS/2, MS-DOS and Windows 3.1 applications through a series of subsystems that provide a protected environment for these applications. System calls are passed on to the WIN32 subsystem which provides the control and support for common system components such as the screen, windows and so on.

The environments are protected in that direct hardware access is not allowed and that a single application will run in a single environment. This means that some applications or combinations may not work in the Windows NT environment. On the other hand, running them in separate isolated environments does prevent them from causing problems with other applications or the operating system software.

Virtual memory manager

The virtual memory manager controls and supervises the memory requirements of an operating system. It allocates to each process a private linear address space of 4 Gbytes which is unique and cannot be accessed by other processes. This is one reason why legacy software such as Windows 3.1 applications run as if they are the only application running.

With each process running in its own address space, the virtual memory manager ensures that the data and code that the process needs to run is located in pages of physical memory and ensures that the correct address translation is performed so that process addresses refer to the physical addresses where the information resides. If the physical memory is all used up, the virtual memory manager will move pages of data and code out to disk and store it in a temporary file. With some physical memory freed up, it can load from disk previously stored information and make it available for a process to use. This operation is closely associated with the scheduling process which is handled within the kernel. For an efficient operating system, it is essential to minimise the swapping out to disk — each disk swap impacts performance — and the most efficient methods involve a close correlation with process priority. Low priority processes are primary targets for moving information out to disk while high priority processes are often locked into memory so that they offer the highest performance and are never swapped out to disk. Processes can make requests to the virtual memory manager to lock pages in memory if needed.

User and Kernel modes

Two modes are used to isolate the kernel and other components of the operating system from any user applications and processes that may be running. This separation dramatically improves the resilience of the operating system. Each mode is given its own addressing space and access to hardware is made through the operating system kernel mode. To allow a user process access, a device driver must be used to isolate and control its access to ensure that no conflict is caused.

The kernel mode processes use the 16 higher real time class priority levels and thus operating system processes will take preference over user applications.

Local procedure call (LPC)

This is responsible for co-ordinating system calls from an application and the WIN32 subsystem. Depending on the type of call and to some extent its memory needs, it is possible for applications to be routed directly to the Local Procedure Call (LPC) without going through the WIN32 subsystem.

The kernel

The kernel is responsible for ensuring the correct operation of all the processes that are running within the system. It provides the synchronisation and scheduling that the system needs. Synchronisation support takes the form of allowing threads to wait until a specific resource is available such as an object, semaphore, an expired counter or other similar entity. While the thread is waiting it is effectively dormant and other threads and processes can be scheduled to execute.

The scheduling procedures use the 32 level priority scheme previously described in this chapter and is used to schedule threads rather than processes. With a process potentially supporting multiple threads, the scheduling operates on a thread basis and not on a process basis as this gives a finer granularity and control. Not scheduling a multi-threaded process would affect several threads which may not be the required outcome. Scheduling on a thread basis gives far more control.

Interrupts and other similar events also pass through the kernel so that it can pre-empt the current thread and re-schedule a higher priority thread to process the interrupt.

File system

Windows NT supports three types of file system and these different file systems can co-exist with each other although they can be some restrictions if they are accessed by non-Windows NT systems across a network for example.

- FAT

  File Allocation Table is the file system used by MS-DOS and Windows 3.1 and uses file names with a 8 character name and a 3 character extension.

- HPFS

  High performance file system is an alternative file system is used by OS/2 and supports file names with 254 characters with virtually none of the character restrictions that the FAT system imposes. It also uses a write caching to disk technique which stores data temporarily in RAM and writes it to disk at a later stage. This frees up an application from waiting until the physical disk write has completed. The physical disk write is performed when the processor is either not heavily loaded or when the cache is full.

- NTFS

  The NT filing system is Windows NT own filing system which conforms to various security recommendation and allows system administrators to restrict access to files and directories within the filing system.

All three filing systems are supported — Windows NT will even truncate and restore file names that are not MS-DOS compatible — and are selected during installation.

Network support

As previously stated, Windows NT supports most major networking protocols and through its multi-tasking capabilities can support several simultaneously using one or more network connections. The drivers that do the actual work are part of the kernel and work closely with the file system and security modules.

I/O support

I/O drivers are also part of the kernel and these provide the link between the user processes and threads and the hardware. MS-DOS and Windows 3.1 drivers are not compatible with Windows NT drivers and one major difference between Windows NT and Windows 3.1 is that not all hardware devices are supported. Typically modern devices and controllers can be used but it is wise to check the existence of a driver before buying a piece of hardware or moving from Windows 3.1 to Windows NT.

HAL approach

The hardware abstraction layer (HAL) is designed to provide portability across different processor based platforms and between single and multi-processor systems. In essence, it defines a piece of virtual hardware that the kernel uses when it needs to access hardware or processor resources. The HAL layer then takes the virtual processor commands and requests and translates them to the actual processor system that it is actually using. This may mean a simple mapping where a Windows NT interrupt level corresponds to a processor hardware interrupt but it can involve a complete emulation of a different processor. Such is the case to support MS-DOS and Windows 3.1 applications where an Intel 80x86 processor is emulated so that Intel instruction set can be run.

With the rest of Windows NT being written in C, a portable high level language, the only additional work to the re-compilation and testing is to write a suitable HAL layer for the processor platform that is being used.

Security

There are two security modules within Windows NT: a subsystem that provides support for applications to use and setup the various levels of security and resource access and a kernel based monitor that ensures that the security provisions and setup are not violated.

Advantages for the user

For the Windows NT user, most of its sophisticated inner workings as previously described are largely hidden from view. For most users, Windows NT looks and feels like Windows 3.1 with the same graphical interface and similar commands and programs. There are several differences however which should not be overlooked.

- Program crashes

  Program crashes are handled differently with Windows NT. If an application crashes within Windows NT, it does not disrupt other applications that are running and therefore allows some recovery to be made. This is made possible through the resource protection that Windows NT uses e.g. separate memory spaces, protected I/O devices and so on. With Windows 3.1, this is not usually the case and an application crash will often bring down the whole system and force the user to restart the system and loose any unsaved data. Pressing CONTROL-ALT-DELETE within Windows NT will display a list of currently running processes — they are called tasks in the dialogue box — and will allow the user to terminate a crashed task without losing or stopping any other running tasks. Anyone who has lost data from a Windows 3.1 crash will appreciate how important and useful this facility is.

- Start up logon procedures

  Windows NT insists on a user logging onto the system before it can be used. This allows the system to be configured for different users in terms of access to files and directories and if connected to the actual network itself. In addition, logging on allows the operating system to audit the user's activities and provides valuable information for calculating who used the system, when and for how long. This information can be used to control and apportion costs for example.

  This is a bit of an overkill for a single user where the auditing information is not really needed

- Shutdown procedures

  With Windows 3.1, Windows is closed and the user returned to the MS-DOS prompt and then the PC can be switched off. Many users simply switch the PC off and while this is not to be recommended because it can potentially damage the file system and the data contained within it, it is a frequently used method. With Windows NT, there is no MS-DOS operating system present because MS-DOS applications run in a simulated environment. As a result, shutting Windows NT will not return to an MS-DOS environment but will present a dialogue box saying that it is safe to turn off the PC. It is important to shutdown Windows NT correctly, and wait for the power off message because it saves and updates the whole file system before the message is presented on screen. If this operation is aborted by switching off the power, data can be lost and in unlucky situations, the file system corrupted.

- Launching multiple copies

    This is a slightly confusing and off putting. Double clicking an icon within Windows NT and Windows 3.1 will open the associated application. If the icon is double clicked again, Windows 3.1 will bring the already open application to the foreground. Windows NT on the other hand will open a second copy of the application. This can be confusing because the application appears but the original documents are missing! In fact, they are not missing but simply associated with the original version of the application.

- Background operation

    Background operation is a little different in that background processes can have a higher priority compared to a foreground task and thus the feel can be slightly different when compared to similar operation under Windows 3.11

- Protected environments

    Some older MS-DOS and Windows software will not run correctly under Windows NT because of the way the software was written. It is possible under MS-DOS and Windows to directly access physical I/O devices and effectively by-pass the operating system software. If this is done within the protected environments provided by Windows NT for MS-DOS and WIN16 (Windows 3.1) applications, then Windows NT will prevent the access and return an error message which inevitably the application cannot handle. The invalid logic behind the software design uses this type of argument: if every PC has a serial port at this address, then I won't get an error message because I will always be able to access it!

2   Installing Windows NT

The installation procedure for Windows NT version 4 is very different from that experienced when installing MS-DOS, Windows 3.1 or Windows '95. The procedure can take a long time — 60 minutes is not uncommon — and not only involves much copying from floppy disk or CD-ROM as any operating system installation requires, but also creates a special set of installation and recovery floppy disks!

CD-ROM or floppy

Windows NT can be installed either from floppy disk or CD-ROM. My advice is to use the CD-ROM even if this means buying a CD-ROM especially for the job. The number of floppy disks involved and the time spent swapping floppy disks is usually more than enough to convince anyone to buy a supported CD-ROM drive.

Before installation

Before installing Windows NT, it is advisable to carry out the following procedures, so that the necessary information and floppy disks are available for the installation.

*   Format four 1.44 MB floppy disks (optional).

    This is optional and not required if the /b option is used with the **Winnt** installation command. Three of the four disks are used during the installation process to create a minimum system specifically for the target system. The fourth disk can optionally be used to create an emergency file system recovery disk.

    The disks must be MS-DOS formatted with nothing stored on them. It is not possible to format the disks during installation or to use blank unformatted disk as they will be rejected.

*   Check that the disk controller(s), CD-ROM drives and interfaces, and graphics controllers are supported by the release of Windows NT or that you have Windows NT drivers to support the hardware.

    This is important because the devices may not have Windows NT support and thus may not be available when Windows NT is booted initially during the installation setup process. This can be a common occurrence with CD-ROM drives. The drive is recognised while the system is running MS-DOS and/or Windows. The initial configuration is setup — minus the CD-ROM drive support — and Windows NT is booted from the startup floppy disks. The MS-DOS CD-ROM driver is naturally lost because MS-DOS is no longer the operating system and Windows NT is now the system software. All well and good except that you can no longer access the CD-ROM and install any additional drivers that are located on the drive!

The solution to this problem is painful: restart the installation making sure that the CD-ROM driver is present or if the Windows NT system is using the NT file system and not the MS-DOS FAT file system, this may require re-installing MS-DOS to get back the access to the CD-ROM drive before re-installing. By the way, re-installation will mean formatting the startup floppy disks again as well.

The moral of this story is check that all the drivers needed to create the minimum system are there and selected during the initial installation process. A common CD-ROM driver that is supported but is hidden away is the SoundBlaster Panasonic CD-ROM interface. This is described and listed as a Panasonic CD-ROM SCSI driver despite the fact that it is not a SCSI interface at all.

• Obtain all the hardware settings for all the devices within the system such as video controllers, sound cards, SCSI drivers and so on.

This should include port addresses, interrupt levels, DMA channels and BIOS ROM addresses if applicable. This hardware information is necessary to configure the hardware and software correctly. Again, if you do not have the correct information available, you may have to re-start the installation process — including re-formatting those three installation floppy disks — after finding out what the settings should be.

It is a good idea to install Windows 3.1 or even Windows '95 and get that working on the final hardware configuration before installing Windows NT. This will enable hardware conflicts over interrupts and so on to be resolved before installing Windows NT. It is quicker to re-install or re-configure Windows 3.1 to sort out these problems and identify a set that has no conflicts than to do the same process with Windows NT.

• Decide on which file system(s) the system will support.

If the system will need to run MS-DOS and/or Windows instead of Windows NT i.e. they are booted up instead of Windows NT, then the file system that contains the associated files must be configured as FAT so that it is accessible by all the operating systems. There is a disadvantage with using the FAT file system in that it does not support all the Windows NT security facilities. However, for many installations including individual workstations that are not networked, this is not a major problem.

If the system needs to run OS/2, then again the file system must be configured so that the disk drives and partitions that contain the OS/2 software and files is either HPFS or FAT. Again, it may be better to install OS/2, not all the hardware settings and then install Windows NT.

In summary, the file system selection will depend very much on what other system will be accessing the files either locally when the alternative operating system is run or remotely across a network.

* Decide on whether Windows 3.1 will be supported and if Windows NT will have access to the Windows 3.1 configuration files.

If Windows 3.1 is installed on the system, it is possible to install Windows NT in the same folder so that the configuration information can be shared. Microsoft's recommendation is to do this, but I am personally unde-cided about this. The case for doing this is that Windows NT can assimilate the Windows information and all the program groups and so on will be transferred. On the other hand, I like keeping operating systems completely separate! I have tried both methods and currently I have installed Windows NT into the Windows 3.1 directory and have experienced no real problems. The only thing that I did have to do was reconstruct some of the program groups the first time I booted Windows 3.1 after the installation.

* Decide on whether Windows '95 will be supported.

The problem with this installation option is that, unlike the case with Windows 3.1, Windows NT version 4 does not pick up the application information from a Windows '95 system and therefore when it is installed, none of the previous applications are recognised or appear in the **Programs** sub-menu.

However, this is not the complete story. Microsoft clearly state in their release notes for Windows NT v4 that it will not pick up any configuration information for applications that were installed under Windows '95. As a result, they recommend a complete re-install of all applications. Through several installation, I have found that this was in fact the case and only by creating program group entries could I restore applications to the Program Group. The moral of this story is clear — be prepared for a major re-installation including all previously loaded applica-tions. This can be a time consuming process to say the least. The alternative is to re-map all the applications manually within Windows NT using the **Settings\\Taskbar** command from the **Start** button. This can also be quite tedious.

If there is a need to share applications between both Windows '95 and Windows NT v4, then either install two versions of the applications using each operating system or install under one and re-create the program groups. There is no real easy solution to this issue yet.

- Decide on the maximum size and location of the swap file.

  If the system only has a single disk and this is configured as a single partition, then the only choice concerns the size of the file. The size is defined as a minimum and a maximum size and should be 2-3 times the amount of physical memory present in the system. A system with 32 Mbytes of RAM would typically have a 60-70 Mbyte swap file.

  The speed of access greatly influences the overall speed of the system: when a command is executed, it may result in pages of data being transferred from RAM to disk and vice versa. The faster this is done the quicker the overall system response will be.

- Backup the system before starting the installation.

  It is possible if the wrong selection is made during the installation to format disks and destroy data. Back it up before starting the installation just in case and make sure that a copy of the backup software is available so that the backups can be used if everything is lost. There is almost nothing more soul destroying than realising that the backup copy is unusable, because the only copy of the backup software necessary to retrieve the data was on the hard disk that has just been formatted.

The installation commands

There are two commands that are used to install the Intel version of Windows NT version 4: **Winnt** and **Winnt32**. **Winnt** is used when installing from MS-DOS and **Winnt32** is used for Windows environments, including upgrading old versions of Windows NT. Both the commands will be found in the same directory that has all the Windows NT files e.g. d:\i386 for Intel systems that have the CD-ROM in drive D.

There are some command options that can change the way the installation is performed. The most important or useful is the /B option which circumvents the long floppy disk preparation and re-boot by transferring the files to a hard disk. This is time consuming but can be done unattended. To use this option simply run the command **Winnt /b** and follow the instructions. Although the /B otion help file — obtained by using the /? option with the command and shown on the facing page — states that the /S option is needed as well, it is sufficient to simply use the /b option to use the floppyless installation. The method will still request a single floppy for an emergency recovery disk.

```
Installs Windows NT.

WINNT [/S[:]sourcepath] [/T[:]tempdrive] [/I[:]inffile]
      [/O[X]] [/X | [/F] [/C]] [/B] [/U[:]scriptfile]]
      [/R[X]:directory]

/S[:]sourcepath
        Specifies the source location of Windows NT files.
        Must be a full path of the form x:\[path] or
        \\server\share[\path].
        The default is the current directory.
/T[:]tempdrive
        Specifies a drive to contain temporary setup files.
        If not specified, Setup will attempt to locate a drive for you.
/I[:]inffile
        Specifies the filename (no path) of the setup information file.
        The default is DOSNET.INF.
/O      Create boot floppies only.
/OX     Create boot floppies for CD-ROM or floppy-based installation.
/X      Do not create the Setup boot floppies.
/F      Do not verify files as they are copied to the Setup boot floppies.
/C      Skip free-space check on the Setup boot floppies you provide.
/B      Floppyless operation (requires /s).
/U      Unattended operation and optional script file (requires /s).
/R      Specifies optional directory to be installed.
/RX     Specifies optional directory to be copied.

To get help one screen at a time, use WINNT /? | MORE
```
The Winnt help window

The installation procedure itself

The installation procedure is fairly straightforward and for the exact detail, please refer to the release notes that are supplied with the software. This section will give an overview of the different phases that are involved.

- Boot up the system with the installed drivers for CD-ROM.

    A minimum system would be MS-DOS and does not need to run Windows NT, Windows '95 or Windows 3.1.

- Insert the installation CD-ROM.

- Locate the directory that holds the files for the processor type that the workstation is using e.g. Intel 80x86, DEC Alpha, MIPS or PowerPC.

- Run the setup program to create the three installation floppy disks.

    The three floppy disks are optional. By using the \b option with the command, the need for the floppy disks is removed. The installation copies all the relevant files on to the system and then boots from there instead. This is the method and option that I normally use. Use **Winnt** to install from MS-DOS and from **Winnt32** Windows. With a Windows based installation, inserting the CD-ROM will bring up a special window with a special installation icon. Clicking this will also start the installation procedure although it is better to use the command directly from the Explorer or File Manager if you want to use one of the options.

- Select the device drivers required for the disk, floppy and CD-ROM drives.

Don't forget that the SoundBlaster/Panasonic CD-ROM driver is listed under the SCSI drivers as a Panasonic CD-ROM. The IDE drivers should also appear in this list and are normally automatically detected. This includes support for IDE and ATAPI CD-ROM drives.

- Restart the system.

  The setup program will normally do this and prompt for the installation of the three floppy disks if the /B option was not used

- Specify hardware parameters as requested to install network connections, printers and so on.

  This is optional and can be completed from within Windows NT after the main installation is completed.

- Specify user and administration names.

  Even if the system is being used as a single user with no connection to other machines, the security system cannot be disabled and will request domain, system and user names and passwords. Fortunately, it will accept blank passwords and almost any text can be used for the various names.

  If the network is not installed, then some of the facilities offered during this part of the installation phase

- Create the emergency recovery floppy disk.

  This is again optional but worth while. Without it, recovering data from a crashed or corrupted system is fairly limited.

Booting Windows NT

The messages that are displayed during the Windows NT boot procedure are different from that experienced with MS-DOS or Windows NT and can be a little off putting if they are not expected.

After the computer is switched on and the BIOS routines have completed, a black window with white text appears entitled the OS Loader. This is the start of the booting procedure and displays three options although others can be added. The first two are concerned with Windows NT and the third usually allows the selection of MS-DOS as the operating system. The first option boots Windows NT as normal. The second option will also boot Windows NT but with the graphics set to the standard VGA and thus override the desktop and graphics controller configurations. This is useful if the monitor of graphics card have been changed. The VGA mode is supported by all cards and once Windows NT has been booted, its configuration can be changed to reflect the new monitor or graphics card using the desktop control panel. The third option will boot MS-DOS and thus allow Windows to be used.

```
OS Loader v4.00

Please select the operating system to start:

Windows NT Workstation v4.00
Windows NT Workstation v4.00 [VGA mode]
MS-DOS

Use ≠ and Ø to move highlight to your choice

Press ENTER to choose.

Seconds until highlighted choice will be started automatically: 28
```
Selecting the OS

The operating system is selected by using the up and down arrow keys to move the highlight. Pressing enter will immediately select the highlighted operating system. However, there is a time limit imposed on the manual selection shown by the decreasing number of seconds in the bottom left of the screen. When the number reaches zero, highlighted operating system will automatically be chosen and the boot procedure will continue. Both the names and the time out duration can be changed by using the system control panel once Windows NT has booted.

```
OS Loader v4.00

Please select the operating system to start:
_____
Windows NT Workstation v4.00
_____
Windows NT Workstation v4.00 [VGA mode]
MS-DOS

Use ↑ and ↓ to move highlight to your choice

Press ENTER to choose.

Seconds until highlighted choice will be started automatically: 28

NT Detect Checking Hardware
```
Hardware checking

The next part of the procedure is where a hardware check is performed and if successful, the OS Loader will continue. At this point, there is an opportunity to select the Windows NT configuration that will be used during the boot procedure. This is shown by the clearing of the screen and the appearance of a message asking for the spacebar to be pressed to access the last known good menu. Again this option is time limited and the time period is short — it is only a few seconds.

If the space bar is not pressed, the boot procedure will continue as normal. If it is, another screen is displayed giving further options.

```
OS Loader v3.51 ...

Press spacebar NOW to load Last Known Good Menu
```
OS Loader message

Configuration Recovery Menu

This menu is an important one as it can be extremely useful in returning the system to a known working state, in the event that configuration changes have caused problems.

The menu gives two additional options to using the current startup configuration. The simplest is to restart the computer and the second is to use the Last Known Good Configuration. This is the settings that Windows NT used correctly and was set by selecting the use current system configuration.

The procedure works in this way: Windows NT keeps a second set of the configuration information as well as the current set. This second set is called the Last Known Good Configuration. The set is created or updated through the successful booting up of Windows NT and when the first user logs onto the system. Logging on not only completes the boot procedure using the current configuration but also updates the Last Known Good Configuration as well.

```
Configuration Recovery Menu (Last Known Good)
This menu allows  you to switch to a previous system configuration
which may overcome system startup problems.

If the system starts correctly now, choose
Use Current Startup Configuration. No change will occur.

If the system does not start correctly
choose Use Last Known Good Configuration

IMPORTANT: System configuration changes made since the last successful
startup will be discarded.
```

```
Use Current Startup Configuration
Use Last Known Good Configuration
Restart the computer

Use the up and down arrow keys to make your selection.
Press enter when you have made your selection.
```
Configuration Recovery Menu

If the 'use the Last Known Good Configuration' option is used instead, the current settings are overwritten with the Last Known Good Configuration and thus will restore a problematic system into a known state. The down side is that any changes that have been made since the Last Known Good Configuration was updated are lost. Using this option can be dangerous because of the potential loss of configuration information that can occur

Using the Configuration Recovery Menu

If Windows NT comes up with problems such as a scrambled video output, then switch off the computer *without* logging on. This will prevent the Last Known Good configuration from being updated. Restart the computer and enter the Configuration Recovery Menu. Select the 'use the Last Known Good Configuration' option and press enter. The system will now use the previous working configuration and overwrite the current configuration and hopefully restore the system to its previous state.

The system check

The last stage in the process is the final system consistency check that is performed which identifies the number of processors and memory installed in the computer and then proceeds to check the file system — this is reminiscent of the file system checks that are performed by UNIX when it starts. The configuration and status information is shown on a royal blue background with white text. Included in this data are the version and build numbers.

If these complete successfully, then the proper Windows NT logo will appear shortly followed by the CONTRL-ALT-DE-

LETE dialogue box inviting a user to press all these keys to start the logon procedure.

```
Microsoft (r) Windows NT (tm) ver 4.00  (build 1357)
1 system processor [ 20,248 kb memory ]
Checking C: drive FAT system
The drive is clean.
Checking D:drive FAT system
The drive is clean
```

Windows NT boot messages

After installation

After a successful installation, the workstation needs to be powered up and checked for correct operation. Logon initially as the administrator so that you have full access to the system. Watch the system for a few minutes because the system will continue to start processes after the logon and therefore a successful logon should not be assumed to be the final confirmation of a successful installation, although it is a pretty good sign.

Typically, any problems should be reported back as an entry in the event log and may be displayed as a warning box as well. Note the message carefully even though it may not make much sense.

Once logged in, check that printers and networks can be accessed. Be patient however as the delay in setting all the services up can cause some accessories and control panels to issue error messages. For example opening the print manager before the print server is running will result in a 'not available' message which can fool you in thinking that there is a major problem with the printer, the print manager or operating system. Before finally tearing your hair out, try opening the print manager several times. When the print server is running, it will open correctly. To see what is happening, use the event viewer in the administrator's program group. This utility will display the state of the operating system and which services and processes have been started up and their current status.

Installation variations

There are some variations to the installation procedure depending on whether Windows NT is pre-loaded or bought as a separate item and the processor type.

On many non-Intel platforms, the Windows NT installation files are pre-loaded onto the hard disk and thus the three floppy disks and CD-ROM (or large number of floppies) are not needed. When the system is powered up, it goes through its normal selftest and BIOS level procedures and then displays the selection menu. Instead of the 'boot Windows NT' option, an 'install Windows NT' message appears. Selecting this will start the installation procedure except that the tiresome procedure of using three pre-formatted floppy disks and so on is by-passed and the files transferred from a partition on the hard disk. The rest of the procedure is as previously described. After the installation, the install option is replaced by the normal 'boot Windows NT' message.

3　　　The Windows '95 shell

Up until the release of Version 4, previous releases of Windows NT used the familiar Windows 3.x graphical user interface (GUI) as the visible interface to the operating system. With the change to Windows '95 and its new and different interface, it was of no surprise that with version 4 of Windows NT, the GUI changed to that of Windows '95. In the early release plans for Windows NT v4, the main development was to the GUI only and not the rest of the system such as the support for the 32 bit APIs like TAPI and so on.

The interface has been available for some time: an alpha version of the Windows NT version 4.0 shell was posted onto the Microsoft Internet site (ftp.microsoft.com) and Microsoft's CompuServe forum for Windows NT version 3.51 in 1995. Needless to say, this software was not officially released and was not supported, but was been provided by Microsoft to allow developers to check their software and to provide a common environment with other Windows '95 based systems, if required.

So what are the differences between this shell and the previous versions? The majority of the applications and techniques described in this book are similar to those found with Windows NT version 3.x: the accessories and control panels are still there and work by and large in the same way. The administrative tools are the same and again work in the same way. What has changed however, is the way that the user accesses and uses the utilities. Given this is the case, what are the differences?

- It provides a Windows '95 compatible desktop and graphical user's interface which replaces the Windows 3.1 shell supplied with versions of Windows NT, prior to version 4.

- The Program Manager is replaced by different tools such as the new Windows NT Explorer that are similar to the Apple MAC interface of a few years ago. Hierarchical menus and pull down tool bar now provide access to programs and files instead of using program groups.

- The File Manager function is augmented by a new utility called My Computer which provides direct access to files and mass storage devices.

- Direct access to network devices is provided by another new utility called Network Neighbourhood which is easy to use to look at files on other systems.

- The windows and associated controls such as minimise, maximise and so on are still present but have a more sophisticated look and feel including the support of 3D features.

- Icons can be put onto the desktop directly. This has some interesting implications for the system. The view provided of the file system is similar to that given by the Apple Macintosh in which the Desktop is the highest point in the hierarchy with all the disk drives, network connections and Desktop files and objects given equal precedence below it. When browsing through the file system, all of these files, directories and objects are visible. This is used by the operating system to create special versions of the Explorer — the File Manager replacement — where only parts of the file system are shown such as the Network connections and so on.

- The Taskbar replaces the task list.

- There is a re-cycling bin to delete files instead of using the delete key or command.

The Windows '95 desktop

The new desktop is radically different from its predecessor. The main control is provided by a combination of a Taskbar and the new utilities on the desktop. The Taskbar provides buttons that represent applications or windows that are running in the system. In this way, they replace the minimised icons that used to be used.

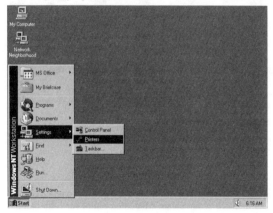

The Windows '95 shell desktop

To bring a window or application to the foreground, the appropriate button is clicked using the cursor to select it and the left hand mouse button. At the right of the Taskbar is a clock and at the left is a button with the Windows symbol. In this release, it indicates that a debugger is present but in the final release this will probably be replaced with the word start, as is the case with Windows '95. Clicking this button activates the Windows NT Explorer or Explorer for short that effectively replaces the Program Manager. It is often referred to as the **Start** button because it is frequently the starting point for accessing a control panel, accessory, application or document.

The Taskbar can be moved by dragging it from one edge of the screen to another. By default it is located at the bottom edge of the screen but in the screenshots shown, it was moved to the top edge of the screen by dragging it upwards.

Window handling

To change the window size, use the same technique as used in the Windows 3.1 shell — move the cursor to the edge of the window where it will change to a double arrow. The arrow's direction indicates in which direction the window can be shrunk or enlarged. To change the size, hold down the mouse button and drag the cursor while still holding down the button. The window will change size accordingly. When the correct size has been created, release the button and the window will adopt the new size.

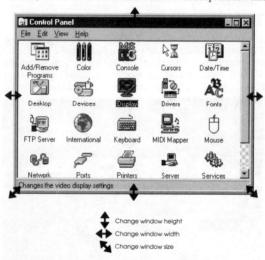

↕ Change window height
↔ Change window width
↘ Change window size

Changing window size

The window can also be moved by the button hold and drag technique. Place the cursor in the coloured title bar — the blue area with Control Panel — press and hold down the mouse button and the window will move without changing size. When it is in the right location, release the button and the window will stay in its new location.

The other control areas are shown in the annotated screen shot. The close window button will close the window and if the window is part of an application, it can be a shortcut to quitting the application itself. The minimise button will reduce the window to a button on the Taskbar itself. Note that with this shell, the window is not reduced to an icon on the desktop! Instead, a tab entry is created on the Taskbar The maximise button will expand the window to the full screen size. If the window already occupies the whole screen, the window will be reduced in size.

Move window

Click here with the
RIGHT mouse button to
display window menu

Maximise window

Close window

Minimise window

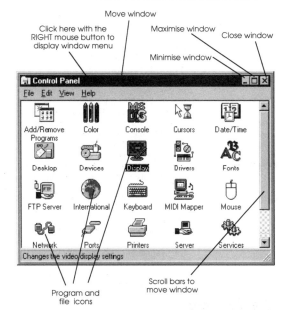

Scroll bars to
move window

Program and
file icons

Other window controls

The window menu

With the Windows 3.1 shell, a single click on the close
window button would display a pull down menu with a set of menu
commands. These commands are still available but are revealed
using a different technique: the cursor is placed on the title bar of
the window — the strip at the top of the window that contains the
window title and the minimise, maximise and close buttons — and
the right hand mouse button pressed and released. The menu will
appear on the screen. This new technique is used with other icons
and applications to get access directly to specific commands
without having to open the application first and then select the
command.

Restore	This will restore the program group, a minimised window or icon to its normal size.
Move	This changes the cursor icon to a multi-pointed arrow which is used to move the windows location. The arrow is placed over the window, the mouse button pressed and held down and the window dragged to its new location. When the mouse button is released, the window is moved to the new location.
Size	This changes the cursor icon to a multi-pointed arrow which is used to change the windows size. The arrow is placed over the

window, the mouse button pressed and held down and the window dragged in the direction of the new size. Moving horizontally will change the width and vertically the height. When the mouse button is released, the window size is changed.

Minimise
This will shrink the current window down to a button on the toolbar. This is useful if the screen is small and there are many applications open. Minimising reduces the screen clutter at the expense of having to minimise the window and then maximising it later. This is the same as clicking on the ▬ button in the title bar.

Maximise
This will expand a window to take the full screen. This is the same as clicking on the ▢ button in the title bar.

Close
This will close the window. This is the same as double clicking the ✕ button on the title bar.

Properties
This allows the properties of the window or application that controls the window to be changed. The dialogue box that appears is specific to the window. Typically, this would be the window attributes such as the font, colours and so on.

The Taskbar

The Taskbar

The Taskbar has effective replaced the Task List as the main method of accessing tasks. It has a permanent task called the Explorer that is designated by the Windows icon and is located on the extreme left of the bar. Other tasks running in the system are located as named buttons to the right of it. When a window is minimised, it does not reduce to an icon, but is allocated a button on the bar. To re-open it or maximise the window, the appropriate button on the Taskbar is clicked. The clock is an optional extra that can be turned off is needed. The **Start** button is the starting point for accessing program groups and so on. In the examples shown, it is the button marked Unicode Debug. In a normal version that is released to users, this name is replaced with Start. The screenshots are from a special developer's version which has special debugging code installed and to identify this version, the name is changed.

The old Task List is not available with this version of the shell and selecting it from the CONTROL–ALT–DELETE dialogue box will activate the Taskbar instead. The normal key sequence of ALT–TAB still functions as expected. The question arises of how can you close a task without the task list? This is solved through the use of the right hand mouse button. By clicking the button on the Taskbar with the right hand mouse button, instead of the left hand one, a menu is displayed that allows the user to close or restore the task associated with the button. By selecting the **Close** command, the task can be removed.

Copying and moving files

Files and directories can be moved, copied and deleted simply by dragging their respective icons onto the icon of the destination to copy or move them or to the recycle bin to delete them. In general, the Windows '95 shell is more flexible on what it allows to be dragged from one window to another. However its operation is not immediately obvious and the decision to move or copy the files or directories depends on the destination and which mouse button is used to click with. The actions are as follows:

The left mouse button

This is the normal operation.

Destination	Action
Same disk	The file is moved.
Different disk	The file is copied using a shortcut.
Same disk	The directory and its contents are moved.
Different disk	The directory and its contents are copied.

The right mouse button

In this case, the file is dragged across using the right hand mouse button instead of the more normal left hand button.

Destination	Action
Same disk	The copy/move menu is displayed.
Different disk	The copy/move menu is displayed.

This operation can be seen in the screen shot. The file AUTOEXEC.000 has been dragged used in the right hand mouse button over the folder called ZIPPRO. The ZIPPRO folder has dimmed to indicate that it has been selected. Releasing the mouse button causes the menu to be displayed which allows the user to select the mode that is to be used to transfer the file. There is one other point: transparent icons are used and if a drag and drop transfer is not possible, a circle with a diagonal bar will appear..

The right hand file transfer menu

Shortcuts

Shortcuts are the equivalent of aliases used within the Apple MAC and UNIX operating systems and are small files that look and act like the original file but do not contain all the file information. Instead they simply have a reference so that if the shortcut is opened, the operating system recognises the fact that it is opening a shortcut, takes and uses the reference to locate the original file and then proceeds to open that instead. The net result is that a single file can be located in many locations without having to have multiple copies of that file. This saves not only disk space but also makes life easy for updates and so on. Updating the original file effectively updates all the shortcuts as well.

The Create Shortcut dialogue box

They can be created as part of the file transfer process as previously described or by selecting the file and using the **File\\Create Shortcut** command. Shortcuts are normally depicted by the addition of a plus sign to their icon.

The Recycle Bin

The Recycle Bin is a new addition to the interface and works just like the Apple MAC wastebasket or trash can does. If a file, directory or group of files are deleted, they are transported to the Recycle Bin. An animated dialogue box then shows the files moving from the folder to the bin. When the files are placed in the bin, they are removed but not deleted.

The deleting... dialogue box

This means that they can be retrieved from the bin if they were put there by mistake. To delete them completely, double click on the bin icon and a window will appear with the contents of the bin displayed. To delete an item, select the item's icon and use **File\\Delete** to delete it.

The Recycle Bin window

To retrieve an item, select its icon and then use the **File\\Restore** to restore it. Items can also be restored by dragging them out of the window and into another window. If the transfer is not possible, a barred circle appears on the screen. To empty the bin completely, use the **File\\Empty Recycle Bin**.

The Windows NT Explorer

The Explorer is the replacement for the Program Manager and provides similar facilities. It allows direct access to its command and so on through a set of hierarchical menus as shown in the screen shot. Some provide direct access to programs and utilities while others allow the desktop to be configured. In addition it also provides an Explorer window which looks like the old File Manager and provides a single window method of navigating through the Desktop and file system. The commands described in the next sections are those available as a set of hierarchical menus from the **Start** button.

The Programs menu

This is the replacement for the old program groups and items. It works by using a special set of folders to hierarchical store links to other directories or files. This special set is located in a directory called Start Menu which can be found in The Windows NT directory. These links are called shortcuts and are the same concept as a program group: they represent a file or directory and contain the command line information and settings necessary to run the application or access the directory. Shortcuts can be added to the Programs menu by selecting **Explorer\\Settings\\Toolbar\\Start Menu Programs**. This displays a dialogue box which allows menu entries to be removed or added to new or existing folders.

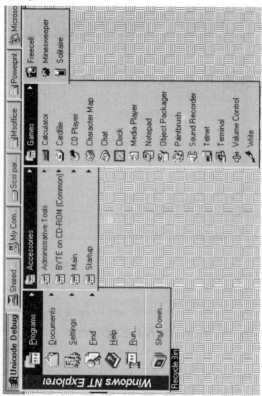

The Windows NT Explorer Programs menu

The Documents menu

The Documents menu keeps a list of the recently used documents and thus allows direct access to them. This is useful if the user is constantly opening the same document. The list can be cleared by selecting **Explorer\\Settings\\Toolbar\\Start Menu Programs**.

The settings options

This menu command gives three options: the first gives immediate access to the Control Panel, the Taskbar configuration software or the Printers control panel. The first two of these options are described later on in this chapter. Printers are described in chapter 8.

Find\\All Files

This utility is used to find files within the filing system by performing a search through the system. It is a more sophisticated directory command and is ideal for searching for files whose name has been forgotten or misplaced. Three dialogue boxes are available to enter the search criteria and these are selected by clicking on the appropriate tab. The first one called Name and Location allows a name or partial name to be entered along with the path names to be searched. The MS-DOS compatible wild card characters such as * and ? are supported as valid entries within the file name, and can be used to search for groups of files that share a common name or part of it.

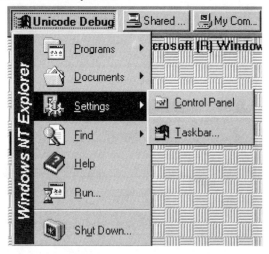

The Windows NT Explorer menu

The Find\ \ All Files dialogue box

The next box allows a range of dates to be specified as criteria and in this way files created or modified within a certain time period can be found.

The advanced options allows specific file and folder types to be defined and their contents searched for data. For example this can be used to search a set of word processor documents for references to a name or other text without having to open them individually.

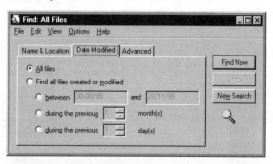

The Find\ \All Files dialogue box

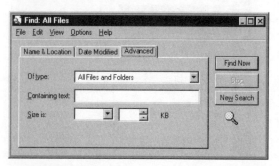

The Find\ \All Files dialogue box

The Find\ \Computer dialogue box

To start the search, click the **Find Now** button. To stop it, click **Stop** button. The **New Search** button can be used to clear all the criteria that are currently being used to search the file system. The results of the search are displayed in an extension to the window. The icons can be opened and moved as required to access the files that meet the criteria that was specified.

Find\\Computer

This utility is similar to the previous one except that the network is searched to find an external computer on the network whose name matches the criteria. This is useful when connected to a large network.

Run

This utility is like its Windows 3.1 predecessors in that it allows an application, folder or file to be opened. Opening a file or application is the same as running it, hence the name of the utility. The target file can be entered directly along with any parameters or it can be selected by using the browse facility by clicking the **Browse** button. The program can be run in its own memory space if needed by clicking the check box below the name box. In most cases, this is already checked as it is the default.

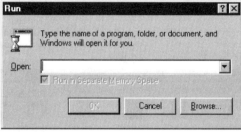

The Run dialogue box

Shutdown

Windows NT does not immediately save all data out to disk and therefore removing power without shutting down and receiving the OK from the operating system is not recommended and risks corrupting the file system and its contents. This command should be used to shutdown the system safely instead of simply switching the power off.

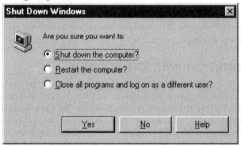

The Shutdown dialogue box

As an alternative, the system can be made to shutdown and then automatically restart. This is useful when installing new drivers for example. This utility allows the user to shutdown the computer, restart it or simply logoff. This last option logs the current user off the computer but does not shut down the machine. This is used when the user wants to end the session but does not or is not allowed to shutdown the machine. Simply select the option required and click the **Yes** button. Pressing the CONTROL–ALT–DELETE keys simultaneously will also display a dialogue box that gives similar options.

The Control Panel

The Control Panel is essentially the same as its predecessor but with the addition of the new look window and an additional utility called Add/Remove Programs which is a utility to install and perhaps more importantly remove programs. This may not work with existing software — it is likely that it will install but not remove applications — and is designed to support new releases of applications. In practice it is actually treated as a special window and is also accessible from the My Computer utility as well. The menus at the top of the window — File, Edit, View, and Help — are common to both the Control Panel window and many other windows, such as those opened through using the My Computer or the Network Neighborhood utilities.

The Control Panel

Common window menus

In the **Start\\Programs** menu, there is an entry for the command Windows NT Explorer and this is how the second version of the Explorer is accessed. In fact, the Explorer in this format is the key interface for Windows NT v4 as it supplies a set of common menus and commands to virtually all windows. This command set controls the operations within the window and its appearance. This is again something new compared to the old Windows 3.1 shell. The menus can be augmented by other commands, so do not be surprised if the menus are slightly different. The basic commands and their actions are as follows:

The File menu

The file menu provides two types of command: the first set are a set of command-line equivalents to the normal drag and drop techniques that can be used to move files and program groups around. The second set are commands that are typically associated with commands such as delete and copy. Included in this set are the Logoff and Shutdown commands which are also available from the top Program Manager menu previously described.

Open	This will open the selected program group or file that is represented by an icon. It is the equivalent of double clicking the icon.
Create Shortcut	This command creates a shortcut of the selected file.
Delete	This displays a dialogue box which asks for the confirmation that you really do want to delete the selected icon.
Rename	This activates the name box below the selected icon and allows the name to be edited or changed.
Properties	This presents the properties dialogue box and varies depending on the window and its associated application.
Close	This will close the window.

The File menu

The Edit menu

This menu is similar to the cut and paste menu found in most applications. It appears in many of the file utilities because it now supports file transfer. Files and/or directories can be cut or copied and then pasted to move files from one part of the file system to another.

Undo	Undoes the last operation.
Cut	Copies the highlighted item to the clipboard and removes it from the window.
Copy	Copies the highlighted item to the clipboard. The window is not changed.
Paste	Inserts the clipboard contents into the window at a point indicated by the cursor.
Paste Shortcut	Creates a shortcut for the file that is stored on the clipboard

Select All   Selects all the items in the window.

Invert Selection Selects all the items that were not previously selected and de-selects those that were.

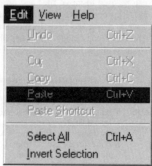

The Edit menu

The View menu

This menu controls the appearance of the data within the window.

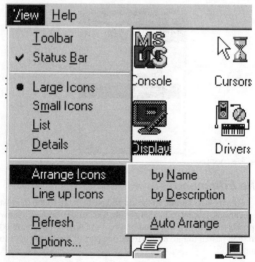

The View menu

Toolbar   This command enables the appearance of the toolbar within the window.

Status Bar   This enables the display of the status bar at the bottom of the window that gives additional information about the current activities or provides descriptions of commands and other information.

Large Icons   This changes the window display to large icons.

Large icons view

Small Icons   This changes the window display to small icons.

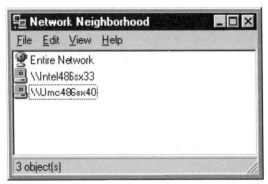

Small icons view

List   This changes the window display to a text list with small icons. To select an item, click on the name not the line.

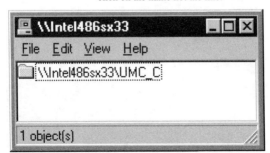

List view

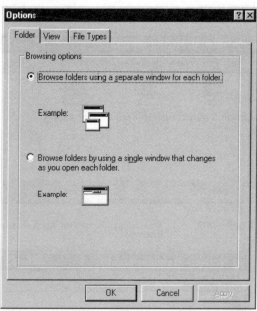

Options dialogue box — Folder

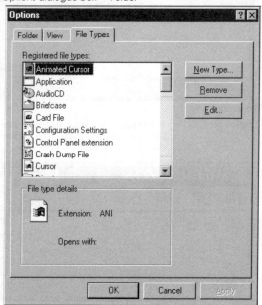

Options diologue box — File types

Details	This changes the window display to a text list with small icons and additional information. Note that the details are not active and an item's name has to be clicked to select it. Clicking on the details associated with the item will not do anything.
Arrange Icons	This command allows the user to arrange the icons automatically without having to manually select each one and move it to its new location.
Line **Up Icons**	This command takes selected icons and lines them up according to the grid parameters that have been defined.
Refresh	This command updates the window contents so that any changes made to the filing system by other applications can be seen.
Options	This displays further dialogue boxes that control or restrict the amount or type of information displayed within the window. Example option dialogue boxes are shown.

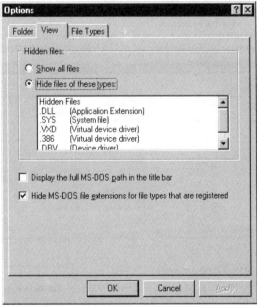

Options dialogue box — View

The Help menu

This menu allows access to the Windows Help system for the utility.

The Explore command

This optional command was included in the Windows NT 3.51 update shell but was omitted in the version 4 release. It has been included for completeness. It was provided by the My Computer and Network Neighborhood utilities and provides a single window for exploring the file system or network.

The command is accessed from the File menu as **File\\Explore** and opens a window with a single partition. It is similar to the Explorer in that one side has a pictorial representation of the file system and the right hand side displays the contents of the selected directory or disk drive. Files and directories can be moved or copied as previously described by dragging from one window to the other, using the right or left hand mouse buttons depending on whether the file is to be moved, copied or represented as a shortcut.

A window opened as a result of using the Explore command is entitled Exploring followed by the name of the parent utility. It is thus possible to have several exploring windows open simultaneously, with a window dedicated to each application.

The utility provides a quick way of using a window to get around the system and is often quicker to use than the alternatives such as the My Computer and Network Neighborhood utilities.

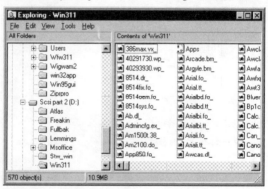

The Explore command window

The Tools menu

These are additional commands that augment the common menu commands available from the window such as File, Edit and so on.

Find
This command allows the user to search through the file system for specific files or directories that match the user's criteria e.g. file name, modification date and so on.

Map Network Drive
This connects to an external network drive and allocates a drive letter to that drive so that it can be accessed and represented within the window. This is similar to the

File Manager **File\\Connect Network Drive**.

Disconnect Network Drive

This command disconnect a network drive.

Go To

This opens a dialogue box that requests the path name of the directory that the user wants to open. If the user knows the full path name, this can be a quicker and easier method of getting to that location.

Taskbar configuration

The Taskbar is the control bar that contains the buttons that represent the Explorer and other applications. It can be moved to a different edge of the screen by simply dragging it to its new location. It is controlled/configured through **Explorer \\ Settings \\ Toolbar \\ Start Menu Programs** which displays one of two dialogue boxes.

Start Menu Programs

This dialogue box allows the user to add or remove items from the hierarchical menus and also to clear the entries in the Documents menu as well. To add items, click the add button and then either enter the full path name of the program or application that is needed along with any command line parameters or alternatively, use the Browser to select a file. The next stage is to decide in which folder the application should be located.

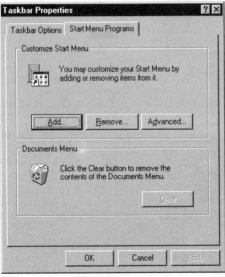

Start Menu Programs

To select the required program folder, simply click on the appropriate icon as displayed in the window. New folders can be created by clicking the **New Folder** button. The folders actually

exist in the Windows NT home directory in a generic folder called
Start Menu. It is possible to move files from one folder to another
within the group manually to re-organise the menus.

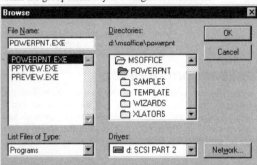

The Browser window

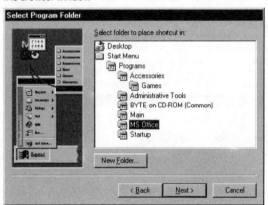

Selecting a folder

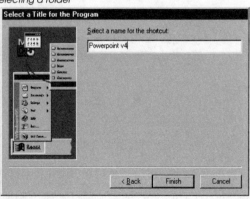

Entering a program title

The final stage is to enter the a name for the entry. This is the name that will appear in the menu. The MS-DOS 8+3 file name convention is not applicable as can be seen from the screen shot. With the name entered, click the **Finish** button to complete the addition.

Removing an entry is similar to the addition procedure and please note that the you can move back to the previous screen to amend names or select a different folder by clicking the **Back** button at the bottom of the window.

Taskbar options

This dialogue box allows the Taskbar to be configured. The first option specifies if the bar is to be always on top of the window when active. The second option will hide the bar until the cursor is placed on the edge of the screen where the bar is located. This will cause the bar to appear and be accessed. The third option defines whether large or small icons are used in the menus and the fourth option will display or hide a clock. Changes to the configuration are visually displayed in the picture in the middle of the window.

Taskbar options dialogue box

My computer

This utility, located on the desktop itself, allows the user to navigate through the file system and manipulate files. It is similar to the File Manager but instead of using separate windows within the application window to represent the files and directories, it creates a separate independent window for each step in the hierarchy. In this way it allows the user to create windows where the user can directly access files and directories.

The window has the common menu items and thus supports different representations of the items within the window: large or small icons can be selected along with various text versions. Double clicking on an directory or disk will open a daughter window that represent the contents of that item. This operation can be repeated as required. Previous windows can be closed thus leaving only the window open for the area of the file system that is off interest.

Files and directories within the windows can be copied and moved by dragging as previously described. Selected items can be deleted by dragging them to the Recycle Bin or using the **File\\Delete** command.

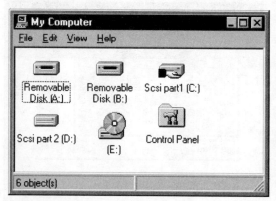

My Computer top window in large icon view

The top window is used to display all the storage devices within the system including any disks that have been accessed through the network. The screen shot shows the two floppy disks, two hard disk partitions and the CD-ROM drive that are installed on the system. In addition, the Control Panel folder is treated as a special case and although physically stored on the C drive, it is displayed in its own right. Selecting **View\\Details** command will display additional information about the devices, such as the free space available and the total storage capacity.

The window supports the standard common menu commands with a few additions: the **File** menu has an **Explore** command that opens up the Explore window.

Opening a disk icon, changes the window to one that looks more like the File Manager. The screen shot show the window with the toolbar enabled where buttons represent the commands that are normally accessed through the menus. The Explore command is now no longer available but in its place a pull down box can be used to obtain a hierarchical representation of the filing system including the components on the desktop. In the screen shot, this is the box that contains the text 'Scsi part1 (C:)'.

My Computer top window in details view

To run an application, simply double click on its icon. To open a document, again, just double click on its icon. In this way, the utility provides windows full off icons that can be opened and manipulated directly without having to go an application such as File Manager.

My Computer drive window

In reality, there appears to be an immense overlap between the My Computer and the Explore utilities/commands, however they do allow the same job to be performed in different ways depending on the user's wishes. The My Computer utility allows a methodical navigation through the file system and allows parts of it i.e. the individual windows to be kept open as individual snapshots. This is useful if you want to move files from one location to another: use My Computer to open windows for each directory and then drag the files from one window to the other. It also provides direct access to common or frequently used parts of the filing system. In this way, the utility is simulating the windows that are used with the Apple MAC interface.

The Explore facility performs a similar job but does so with only a single window and in this way can be more efficient to use, especially if searching through a deeply nested file structure. It does not create the large number of windows that the My Computer utility does. It is more closely related to the File Manager and Program Manager in the way that it allows the user to move through the system.

Properties

With an item selected it is possible to configure or obtain further information about it by using the **File\\Properties** command. The next three screen shots show the information that can be obtained for the disk drive C: by using this command. The dialogue box has three parts describing the sharing, general and tool status.

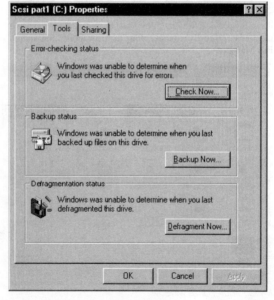

Disk drive properties

The sharing information is similar to that obtained from the File Manager and controls whether the drive is shareable and its shared name. Permissions and other settings can also be set by using the appropriate buttons. This is not quite as all encompassing as the File Manger but for most users provides easier access to the facilities that are most used.

The tools information similar returns when the drive was last backed up, de-fragmented and error checked. This is similar to the

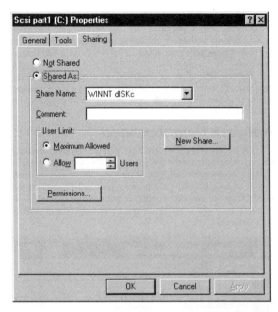

Disk drive properties

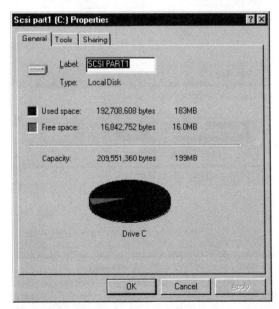

Disk drive properties

facilities found in the administration tools. The general information allows the drive label to be changed and gives information about the disk utilisation and free space. Again, this is a subset of the information available from the disk administration tools.

The properties that are displayed are dependent on the file type and will be different depending on whether it is a document, an applications, an MS-DOS application, directory or as in this case, a disk drive.

Network Neighborhood

This utility is similar to the My Computer utility except that instead of working on the file system, it allows a user to browse through the network and look at files and directories on other servers and workstations. IN this way, it saves having to use the File Manager to manually connect to a drive before being able to examine its contents. As a result, it is a very quick way of looking at the network.

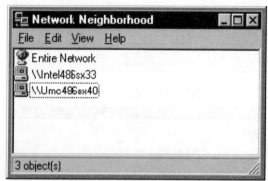

The Network Neighborhood top window

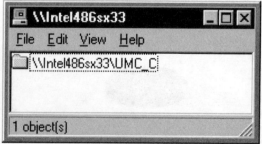

The next Network Neighborhood window

The network drive is selected by clicking on the computers displayed in the window and then selecting from the subsequent window, the drive to be examined. In selecting the drive, the system automatically connects to the drive and then presents its content as a window. Naturally, this means that the user must have the correct permissions and rights. Assuming this is the case, the contents are directly accessible. The utility also supports the Explore command as well.

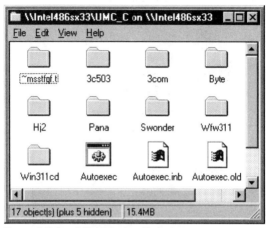

The next Network Neighborhood window

Other right hand button tricks

Clicking on the desktop

A right hand click on the desktop and release displays a menu that allows the user to configure the desktop. The icons that are stored on the desktop can be aligned, moved or pasted. New items can be created as shown in the screen shot. The Properties command actually displays the Colour Control Panel and allows the Desktop colour scheme to be changed.

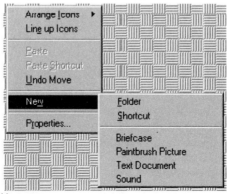

Desktop menu

Clicking on an icon

Similarly, right hand click and release while the cursor is over an icon will display a menu that contains a subset of its commands and thus allow direct access to the commands without having to open the utility and select them from the menu.

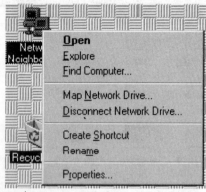

My Computer menu

4   Accessories

The accessories work group contain, like within Windows 3. and previous versions of Windows NT, useful simple applications that exploit the facilities provided within Windows NT environment. Many are similar to their Windows 3.1 counterparts and while knowledge of how these and previous versions work will undoubtedly help, there are some differences and even some new additions to the collection.

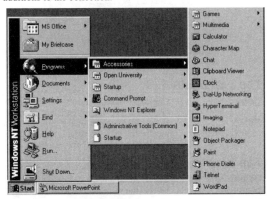

The Accessories window group

The accessories are accessed via the Start button at the left of the Taskbar. Click on the button and a hierarchical menu appears The accessories group is located under the **Program** group. With the accessories menu, there are two additional sub-menus which give access to the games that are shipped with version 4 (including an amazing 3D pinball simulation) and the multimedia group which contains the CD player, Sound Recorder, Multimedia Player and Volume Control.

It is possible to move the location of the accessories group to a different position within the hierarchical menu by changing the Taskbar settings. If this has been done, it may be necessary to search through the all the other menus to find the accessories.

Calculator

Calculator provides a simple calculator on screen and provides the ability to copy and paste numbers directly to and from the display. To do this use the commands in the **Edit** menu. There are in fact two types of calculator available which can be selected by pulling down the **View** menu. The default is the standard four function plus calculator shown below. The other option is a full scientific calculator.

The keys are self explanatory and are similar to those found within a normal calculator except for the back key which will delete the last entered number. It saves using the CE key and re-entering the replacement number.

The standard calculator

The Edit menu

Copy Copies the highlighted text or object to the clipboard. The document is not changed.

Paste Inserts the contents of the clipboard into the document at the point indicated by the cursor or highlighted text or object.

The View menu

Scientific Selects the scientific calculator.
Standard Selects the standard calculator

The Help menu

Help topics This is the menu command to access the on-line help utility.

About Calculator This provides information about Calculator such as the revision number, licensee and so on.

Clock

Clock provides either an analogue or digital clock to be displayed in its own window. The **settings** menu allows the user to select the clock type. The data and time are taken from the system clock. To change the date or time, the date/time control panel is used instead.

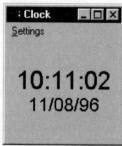

The digital clock

The Settings menu

Analog	This selects the analogue clock with the circular face and moving hands.
Digital	This selects the digital alternative.
Set **F**ont	This is enabled if the digital option is selected and allows the font to be changed.
GMT	Changes the time zone to GMT from the local time and vice versa.
No title	Removes the title bar giving a simple window. The title bar can be brought back by clicking at the top of the window where the bar is normally located.
Seconds	If selected, the clock will display seconds.
Date	If selected, the clock will display the current system date.
A**b**out Clock	This provides information about Calculator such as the revision number, licensee and so on.

Cardfile

Cardfile is a simple database that resembles the old, tried and tested index card system. It replicates a card onscreen into which data — usually text — can be placed for later retrieval. It has a simple search utility that allows cards to be found based on their contents. Although simple, it is ideal for simple jobs such as contact and component lists, telephone and address information and anything that can be put on a card. It was included in version 3.51 but not with version 4. If you are a user, then you will need to transfer the application to continue using it.

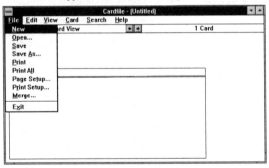

The Cardfile window

The File menu

New	Creates a new file.
Open	Opens an existing file.
Save	Saves the current file. If the file has not been saved before, a dialogue box asking for the new file name will appear.
Save **A**s	Saves the current file with a different file name.
Print	Print the current record.

Print All	Print all the records.
Page setup	Set up page size and other related information.
Print setup	Set up print options such as paper orientation, print quality and other printer specific choices..
Merge	Merge the cards in the current open file with another file. This allows cards from one file to be added to other files without having to re-enter all the data or manually cut and paste from one card to another.
Exit	Quit the accessory.

The Edit menu

Undo	Undoes the last operation.
Cut	Copies the highlighted text or object to the clipboard and removes it from the document.
Copy	Copies the highlighted text or object to the clipboard. The document is not changed.
Paste	Inserts the contents of the clipboard into the document at the point indicated by the cursor or highlighted text or object.
Paste Link	Inserts the contents of the clipboard into the document at the point indicated by the cursor or highlighted text or object. It also creates a special link back to the source of the material. If the source is modified, then the pasted information in this file is automatically updated.
Paste Special	Inserts the contents of the clipboard into the document at the point indicated by the cursor or highlighted text or object. With this paste option, certain aspects of the data can be pasted. For example, the data only without any formatting information. Text can be pasted as a graphical object, formats can be pasted without the original data and so on.
Index	This presents a dialogue box where the card index entry — think of it as a title or serial number or both — that is used to reference the card when using the goto search command.
Restore	This command will restore the current card's contents to that stored in the file. This is useful if you want to undo the changes made to a card. It will only work providing that card is still current and the cards have not been saved back to disk. IN either case, if this is not done, the file is automatically updated and the restore command will not be able to extract the previous version from the file. The file will have been updated and the its card contents and that shown on the screen will be the same.
Text	This indicates the card's contents is text. If this is not selected and the card contains text, it will be impossible to place a cursor

	on the text to highlight or change it. This can be used to lock the card's contents from change. Enter the text and then change the type from text to picture using the next command.
Picture	This indicates if the card's contents is a picture. This needs to be selected to allow an object to be inserted into the card's record.
Link	This allows access to the object linking facilities.
Object	This command is used to create or locate an object which can be inserted into a card using the **Insert Object** command.
Insert object	This allows the insertion of a specific object such as a drawing, graph or spread sheet. It normally requires the Picture option to be selected.
Set Font	This allows the font to be changed.

The View menu

Card	This displays the records as a set of cards with the index at the top and the contents below. The current card can be selected by clicking on it.
List	This displays the index entry for each card as a list. A card can be selected by clicking on it. Double clicking will allow the entry to be modified.

The Card menu

Add	This adds a blank card to the current set.
Delete	This deletes the current card from the set.
Duplicate	This duplicates the current card and adds the duplicate to the set.
Autodial	This allows a telephone number to be dialled using an external modem or autodialler. It will display a dialogue box which allows a number to be entered and the serial port that the autodialler is connected to be setup.

The Autodial dialogue box

	If some text is highlighted before selecting this command, the text is automatically transferred to the dialogue box. This is useful if the card contains a telephone number: simply highlight the number, select the autodial command and click the OK button. The downside is that this com-

mand needs a special autodialler or modem that supports a telephone handset.

The Search Menu

GoTo

This will select a card using the card's index entry. It requests the data that it will search the index entries against to locate the required card.

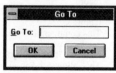

The Goto dialogue box

Find

This is another search facility except that instead of using the index entries, it examines the contents. Again, it will request the text that it will use as its search criteria.

Find Next

This continues a search as defined by Find, so that other matching cards can be located.

The Help menu

Contents

This accesses the Windows NT help utility.

Search for help on

This also accesses the utility but asks for a topic to search for.

How to use help

This is the help utility for the help utility!

About Calculator

This provides information about cardfile such as the revision number, licensee and so on.

Notepad

This is as its name suggests, a simple electronic notepad that can be used to jot down information or even act as a very simple word processor (Write would be a better option as it has more facilities and supports different fonts and so on).

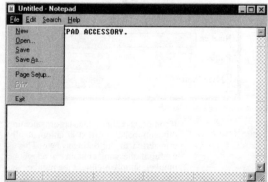

The Notepad window

The File menu

New	Creates a new file.
Open	Opens an existing file.
Save	Saves the current file. If the file has not been saved before, a dialogue box asking for the new file name will appear.
Save As	Saves the current file with a different file name.
Page setup	Set up page size and other related information.
Print	Print the current file.
Exit	Quit the accessory.

The Edit menu

Undo	Undoes the last operation.
Cut	Copies the highlighted text or object to the clipboard and removes it from the document.
Copy	Copies the highlighted text or object to the clipboard. The document is not changed.
Paste	Inserts the contents of the clipboard into the document at the point indicated by the cursor or highlighted text or object.
Delete	Deletes The highlighted text or and removes it from the document.
Select All	This will select/highlight all whole contents of the document.
Time/Date	This will insert the current system time and date into the document where the cursor is positioned.
Word wrap	This enables the word wrap option where the text will automatically continued on the next line when it reaches the right hand margin. If this option is disabled, the window width is simply expanded until either the RETURN key or ENTER key is pressed. The horizontal scroll bar at the bottom of the Window is used to shift the window left or right as required.
Set Font	This sets the font that is used in the display window.

The Search menu

Find	This is a search facility for locating text within the document. It will request the text that it will use as its search criteria.
Find Next F3	This continues a search as defined by Find, so that other matching cards can be located. Pressing the F3 key will also continue the search in the same way.

The Help menu

Help topics	This accesses the help utility.
About Notepad	This provides information about Notepad such as the revision number, licensee and so on.

Paint

The previous versions of Windows NT supplied a paint program called Paintbrush which was a simple bit orientated drawing program that can allow bit mapped drawings to be manipulated and created. Version 4 also supplies a similar program called Paint which has a slightly different user interface. It is simple to use and has most of the basic functions without going to the extreme level offered by dedicated drawing programs. One good use for it is in manipulating and creating wallpaper and desktop patterns.

The icons on the left hand side represent the basic tools that are available. The colour palette shows the colours that are available and by clicking on one of the boxes, that colour is used with the tools. If the click is made with the lefthand button, the *foreground* colour is changed. If the click is made with the righthand button, the *background* colour is changed instead. The currently selected colours are shown on their own to the left of the palette.

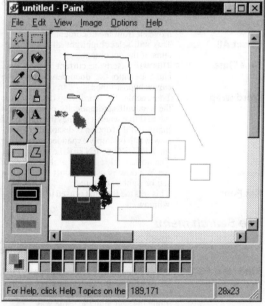

The Paintwindow

The line widths that can be used are depicted in the box at the bottom left. The box will only appear when the line tool is selected, but the selected width will be used with any subsequent tool that uses an outline such as the rectangle or oval tool. Clicking a line will select that width. The current width selection is indicated by the arrow.

A couple of points to remember about Paint: it is a bit mapped drawing program and the boxes, circles and so on that can be drawn are depicted as a bit map. If the picture is enlarged or shrunk, the edges will become ragged as the resolution becomes a problem. This also means that text cannot be modified once it has been put into the picture.

The File menu

New	Creates a new Paint file (the default file extension is .bmp).
Open	Opens an existing Paint file.
Save	Saves the current file. If the file has not been saved before, a dialogue box asking for the new file name will appear.
Save As	Saves the current file with a different file name.
Print preview	Dispaly the printed page on screen before printing.
Page setup	Set up page size and other related information.
Print	Print the current file.
Send	Sends a picture by electronic mail or by fax.
Set as wallpaper(tiled)	
	This uses the picture as wallpaper but tiling multiple copies across the screen to fill it.
Set as wallpaper(centred)	
	This uses the picture as wallpaper but with only a single copy placed in the centre of the screen.
Recent file	This contains a list of recent file names that the application has used.
Exit	Quit the Paint accessory.

The Edit menu

Undo	Undoes the last operation.
Repeat	Repeats the last operation. This is the opposite of the **Undo** command.
Cut	Copies the selected picture to the clipboard and removes it from the document.
Copy	Copies the selected picture to the clipboard. The document is not changed.
Paste	Inserts the contents of the clipboard into the document at the point indicated by the cursor or highlighted text or object.
Clear selection	This command will remove and clear any images(s) within the selected area. If this is executed by mistake, use the **Undo** command to restore the image.
Select All	This command selects the whole picture.
Copy to	This command copies the selected picture to a bit map file. A dialogue box is opened that allows the file's name, location and the number of colours to be used to be defined. Once the picture has been saved as a bit map file — the default file extension is .bmp — it can be used as the screen

| | background or wallpaper. This can also be done directly through the two **Set as Wallpaper** commands in the **File** menu. The desktop control panel is used to set this up. |
| **Paste from** | Pastes the contents of a bit map file to the picture. A dialogue box is opened that allows the file's name, location and the number of colours to be used to be defined. Once the picture has been pasted, it is automatically selected and can be dragged anywhere in the picture. |

The View menu

Tool Box	If selected, the tool box is displayed. If not, it is hidden.
Color Box	If selected, the color box is displayed. If not, it is hidden.
Status Bar	If selected, the status bar is displayed. If not, it is hidden.
Zoom	This will present a sub-menu which gives the following options:
Normal size	Sets the picture to the normal size.
Large size	Magnifies the picture.
Custom	Allows a custom value to be used for increasing or decreasing the picture size.
Show Grid	If selected displays an alignment grid on the picture.
Show Thumbnail	Displays a thumbnail version of the picture.
View Bitmap	This will display the picture using the complete window. All the palettes, tool bars and so on are removed so that as much of the picture can be seen as possible. Drawing is not allowed in this mode. Clicking the mouse button will restore the palettes and tool bars as before.
Text toolbar	If selected, the text toolbar is displayed when the text tool is used. This allows the font, its size and other effects to be selected. If this option is not selected, then the default setting is used instead.

The Image menu

This menu is dimmed out and not available until part of the picture has been selected to create a what is known as a cut-out. It provides the ability of manipulate a cut out and control its attributes such as colour depth and so on.

Image	Options	Help
Flip/Rotate...	Ctrl+R	
Stretch/Skew...	Ctrl+W	
Invert Colors	Ctrl+I	
Attributes...	Ctrl+E	
Clear Image	Ctrl+Shft+N	

Flip/rotate
This will present a dialogue box that will allow the cut-out to be either flipped horizontally or vertically, or to be rotated. With a horizontal flip, the cut-out so that the right-hand side becomes the left hand side and vice versa. With a vertical flip, this will flip the cut-out so that the top becomes the bottom and vice versa. Rotation allows the cut-out to be rotated either by 90 degrees or some other variable figure. Rotating by 90 degrees will convert a landscape picture to portrait and vice versa and is useful when the cutout is to wide to fit across the page.

Stretch/Skew
This gives another dialogue box that allows the selected image to be manipulated in one of two ways:
The stretch option allows the cut-out to be increased or decreased in size. The second option allows the cut-out to be tilted or skewed e.g. a rectangle can turned into a parallelogram.

Invert colors
Inverts the colours within the cut-out so that white becomes black and vice versa.

Attributes
This command displays a dialogue box where the picture size can be changed or defined. In addition, the default measurement unit i.e. inches, centimetres or pels (pixel elements) can be selected. The picture can be defined to use black and white or colour.

Clear Image
This command will change the colour used for the background of the cut-out to that of the picture background colour.

The Options menu

This menu provides the commands that control the colours that are available to the tools within the program.

Edit Colors
This allows the colour palette to be edited. A dialogue box appears with three sliders that allow the currently selected colour to be adjusted. Dragging the sliders alters the colour blend and the colour can be adjusted. Where the old colour has been used in the drawing, it will remain unchanged. In this way, it is possible to use many more colours than the palette shows. By changing the palette, hundreds of colours can be used in the drawing.

Get Colors
This fetches a colour palette from a file.

Save Colors
This saves the colour palette to a file for later use.

Draw opaque
This selects the drawing mode. In the opaque mode, any new drawing will cover the existing image that is underneath it using foreground and background colours. If not selected, the transparent mode is used, the underlying image will show through.

The Help menu

Help topics
This accesses the help utility.

About Paint
This provides information about Paint such as the revision number, licensee and so on.

Chat

This is a new utility and it allows conversations between the host PC and any other on the network. A conversation is carried out through the interactive typing and display of text between the two parties. It is similar to using a bulletin board or participating in an interactive user group except that the chat takes place between two parties.

Any PC that wants to participate, must have a working network connection in place and a chat is setup by selecting a PC on the network using the select computer dialogue box.

HyperTerminal

This is the successor to Terminal and is probably the most used accessory for anyone with a modem. It provides a terminal emulation and file transfer facility between the host PC and any other PC, workstation or mainframe. It requires that the other party supports either multiple users with their own terminal or links via a serial line of some kind. Providing the other PC — often known as a remote party or host — has similar terminal emulation software running, this accessory can even transfer files between the incompatible computers as well.

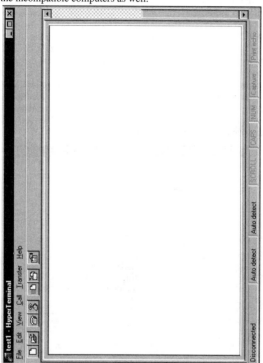

The Terminal window

One of the main differences between it and its predecessor, Terminal, is that HyperTerminal uses the TAPI(Telephony Application Programming Interface) interface to access modems that are attached to the PC. In this way, the attachment and configuration of a modem is not handled by HyperTerminal directly but through the Telephony control panel. If the accessory is opened with no modem or other information, it will request that information initially. It is important to remember that a modem configuration cannot be changed or a different modem added through HyperTerminal afterwards. What happens is that HyperTerminal calls the Telephony control panel and it appears as if the accessory is in control of everything. It is not: user information can be changed from within the accessory but adding more or different modems to TAPI's registered list cannot be done.

The accessory works by saving profile information for a connection. This can be stored and simply opened to access a particular service. In building up the profile, the accessory starts initially by asking information about the telephone link that you have e.g. the local telephone code, country, numbers to access direct lines and so on. It then proceeds to check if any modems have been installed. As a result, what was the Terminal settings information is now split into several sections: the first is the modem link where the modem type is recognised and configured, including the port it is attached to. The second section in the configuration information that contains details about the call and connection itself. The two are referenced through the use of a modem name which links the two sections together. The modem information can be used and referenced by as many connection files as needed. If the modem need to be changed to a different port, the modem configuration can do this without having to change all the other connection files. With the Terminal settings approach, each setting would need changing.

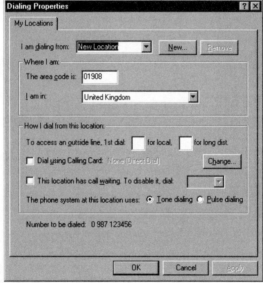

The Dialling Properties box

There is also a third section which is handled by TAPI which is the location information. This allows a user to specify the additional connection information to access an outside line, international dialling codes and so on so that instead of modifying the telephone number or Terminal setting, a different location is used instead. This is known as the Dialling Properties.

There are other differences: the fine control that Terminal gave you concerning the terminal setup and function keys is not present. The set up can also be a little mystifying with the information essentially split between two entities. The advantage is that a lot of the detection and setup is now automatic and therefore the need for control in many cases does go away.

Installing a modem

If no modem has been installed via the Telephony control panel, then this will be done automatically. The first stage is to ask for the intial settings for a location via the Dialling Properties dialogue box. An example is shown on the previous page. This is covered in more detail later in the section on the **Connect** command. Essentially, this defines how to dial from this location. It is recommended that you change the location name to something meaningful. You can also create multiple locations at this point as well. If the PC is a portable, a location for the home, the office and any other remote locations would be a good idea.

Once this information is filled in, a modem installation dialogue appears. There is a wizard available that guides you through the process and gives you two choices: either let the system automatically detect the modem or alternatively, you can choose it from a list. If the modem is not on the list, it is usually possible to choose either a generic type — Hayes compatible for example — or one that is similar.

The automatic detection can take some time — several minutes is not uncommon — and needs the modem to be connected and switched on. Failure to do either of these operations can cause the auto-detection to fail and the message that no modem was detected. With a built-in modem, this is less likely to happen.

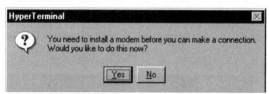

The modem install dialogue

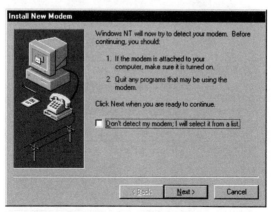

The modem install wizard

Creating a connection

The connection information completes all the settings and is where the host telephone number is entered and other details about the link are set up. This information can be saved and opened again by using the appropriate commands from the **File** menu.

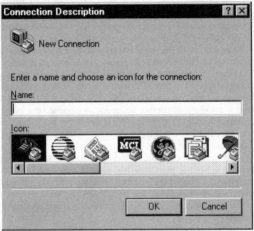

The connection dialogue box

The first part is to name the connection and define the icon that it will use in the window and task list. Typically, the name should refer to the service or host that is being connected to. The icon is used instead of the default for easy identication as well.

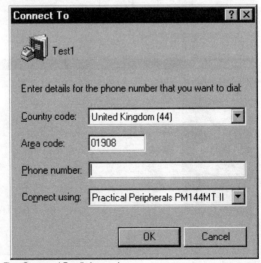

The Connect To dialogue box

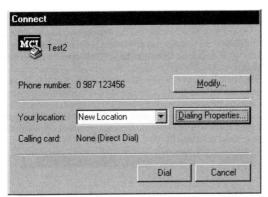

The Connect dialogue box

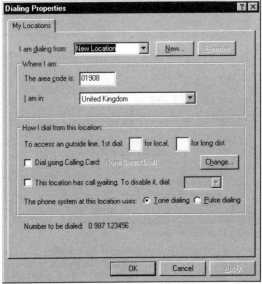

The Dialling Properties box

The next dialogue box requests the details of the telephone number that is to be used. The third dialogue box is used to select the location that is used to complete the telephone details i.e. the number to get an outside line and so on. If everything is correct, the **DIAL** button can be clicked to start the connection. The **Cancel** button will terminate the connection.

At this point is is possible to change the dialling properties by clicking on the appropriate button to display the dialogue box. This should be done if the location(s) are not suitable e.g. there is a different number for an ouside line or alternatively the call is being made internationally.

Changing a connection

To change a connection, use the **Properties** command from
the **FILE** menu and this will display the properties dialogue box.
This has two options: **Connect to** and **Settings**. The **Connect
to** box allows the details about the call such as area code and
telephone number to be defined as well as which device or serial
port is to be used. In the example shown, this has been set to a
Practical Peripherals modem which was installed previously. The
modem can also be configured by clicking on the **Configure**
button which will allow the transfer rates and other information to
be defined or changed.

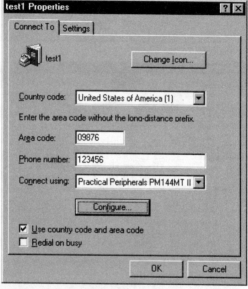

The connection properties

This part of the properties defines the communications protocol itself. The computer typically has several serial ports,
COM1, COM2 and so on which are used to transfer data between
the PC and printers, modems and even other computers. The term
'serial' comes from the fact that only one data line is used to
transmit and receive data and thus the information must be sent
and received a bit at a time. Instead of transmitting the 8 bits that
make up a byte using 8 data lines at once, one data line is used to
send 8 bits, one at a time.

The serial interface can be divided into two areas. The first is
the physical interface, commonly referred to as RS-232 or EIA-
232, which is used to transfer data between the terminal and the
computer. It is important to get its settings right, as they form the
basis of all future communication. The second area controls the
flow of information between the terminal and computer so that

neither is swamped with data it cannot handle. Again, failure to get this right can cause data corruption and other problems. The port's settings can be changed using this command

When a user presses a key, quite a lengthy procedure is carried out before the character is transmitted. The pressed key generates a specific code which represents the letter or other character. This is converted to a bit pattern for transmission down the serial line via the serial port on the computer system. The converted bit pattern may contain a number of start bits, a number of bits (5, 6, 7 or 8) representing the data, a parity bit for error checking and a number of stop bits. These are all sent down the serial line by a UART (universal asynchronous receiver transmitter) in the terminal at a predetermined speed or baud rate.

Both the computer and the peripheral it is communicating with, must use the same baud rate and the same combination of start, stop, data and parity bits to ensure correct communication. If different combinations are used, bits will be wrongly interpreted. The result is garbage on the screen and an extremely confused computer! Up to this point, there is no visual confirmation on the display that the key pressed has resulted in the transmission of a character.

If the terminal UART is configured in half duplex mode, it echoes the transmitted character so it can be seen on the screen. Once the data is received at the other end, it is read in by another UART and, if this UART is set up to echo the character, it sends it back to the terminal. (If both UARTs are set up to echo, double characters appear on the screen!) The character is checked by the operating system software, against a list of special characters which perform operations such as backspace, clearing command lines and interrupting commands during their execution. If it is not a special character or a carriage return, the character is placed in a buffer where it stays until a carriage return is received. The advantage of buffered input is that the user can type commands ahead while waiting for the current command to complete. Once the carriage return character is received, the characters in the buffer are flushed out and passed to the shell or application to process. The buffer is thus emptied.

Serial bit stream

	0, 1 or 2 start bits
	5,6,7 or 8 data bits
	Odd, even or no parity bit
	0,1 or 2 stop bits

Serial bit streams

Parity Check is an option where the parity bits if enabled are actually checked with the data. This is usually not performed as other protocols such as Kermit and Xmodem can detect errors far more efficiently. The **Wait for dial tone** or carrier detect is an option that will make sure that the modem is connected to a valid line and that it is ready to work. The term is also applicable to one of the RS-232 signals. If this signal is not supported — and it often in not used — checking this box will stop an otherwise good link from working.

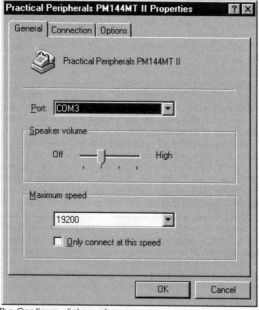

The Configure dialogue box

The General panel within the dialogue box is where the connection speed is set. Note that it is a maximum value and dependent on the line quality. The modems will negotiate and work out the highest rate that they can support. The serial port that is to be used is also displayed and this can also be changed. The speaker volume refers to the level used when playing the initial dialling tones and other noises that are encountered when making the connection.

If the volume is turned off, it can be difficult to know if the call is actually being dialled and if their is a dialling tone. It also prevents any messages that the telephone company might send indicating that a number has changed or is unavailable. If the volume is too high, it can simply be very annoying especially if the PC's speaker output is via a couple of high powered speakers used for multimedia playback. In this example, a low level is used and this is ideal in most cases.

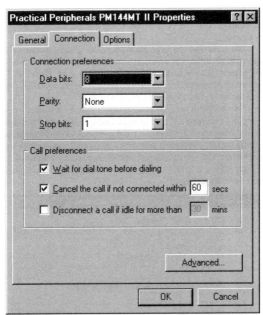

The Connection panel

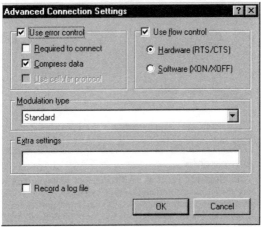

The advanced settings dialogue box

The Connection panels sets up the data, parity and stop bits and also defines any call preferences. The Wait for dial tone option is used when going through a PABX where there may be a delay or even uncertainty about getting a dialling tone. If it is disabled, then the dialling will go through automatically —useful when the local dial tone is different from normal and is not recognised by the modem. This can be the case when dialling in from remote locations.

The advanced settings allow data compression and flow control to be defined as well as the modulation standard. A fourth box is provided for additional settings in terms of Hayes (AT) command strings to be entered. The Hayes command strings and their meanings are defined in Appendix A.

Another point to be aware of is that Windows NT allows you to create serial ports e.g. COM3 and COM4 which cannot be used. Unlike Windows 3.1, version 3.5 and version 3.51 do not let serial ports share interrupt levels and although the additional ports exist and have valid names, the drivers do not work! Version 4 is slightly different in that they may work but strange system lock ups can be experienced!

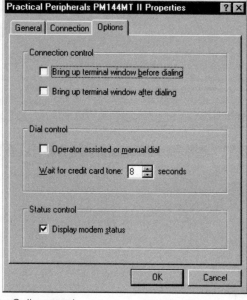

The Options panel

The **Settings** panel of the **Properties dialogue box is where** the terminal configuration to be adjusted. Traditionally, this is where information such as the terminal emulation required, whether line wrap is switched on and so on is defined. With HyperTerminal, much of this is done automatically through its automatic terminal emulation facility. The various terminal modes indicate whether line wrap — where lines are automatically truncated by carriage returns to fit the terminal column width — is supported, whether the characters sent to the remote party are also displayed on screen so that they can be seen, and whether beeps and other sounds are enabled or disabled. The local error option within the ASCII setup dialogue box can cause double characters to appear e.g. ccaatt instead of cat. If this happens, try disabling this option.

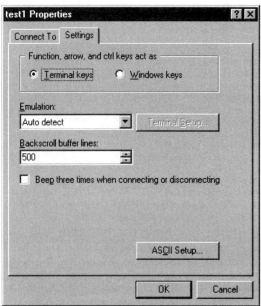

The Setting dialogue box

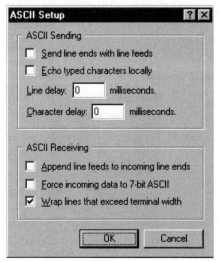

The ASCII setup dialogue box

The number of characters that the terminal will display in a row can be changed by changing the terminal emulation. In the example, this is set to Auto detect, but by using the drop down menu other terminal configurations can be selected. Each one can be further configured by clicking on the **Terminal Configuration** button along side the drop down menu.

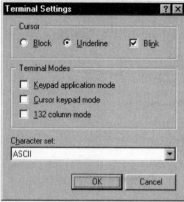

The VT100 terminal configuration dialogue box

The font and font size used in the window cannot be changed here but instead is modified by using the **Font** command in the **View** menu. The size of the buffer and the ability to scroll through the buffer is also modified through this panel. The **ASCII setup** button leads to another dialogue box . These final options allow some forms of translation between IBM and ANSI character sets, different international characters and whether a return or enter key should generate a carriage return with or without a line feed. If no line feed is generated and the remote party expects one, then each new line will overwrite the preceding line without moving down the window.

The File menu

This menu controls the opening, closing, modification and saving of connection files as well as the printing of data from the screen.

New	Creates a new file — this creates a new connection to a different remote location.
Open	Opens an existing file. This retrieves the connection information that had previously been saved.
Save	Saves the current file. If the file has not been saved before, a dialogue box asking for the new file name will appear. This effectively saves the connection information.
Save **A**s	Saves the current file with a different file name.
Page set**u**p	Set up print options such as paper orientation, print quality and other printer specific choices.
Print	Print the current screen.
P**r**operties	Change the current connection properties. This is explained in detail after the next command.
E**x**it	Quit the accessory.

The Edit menu

| **C**opy | Copies the highlighted text within the display window to the clipboard. The document is not changed. |
| **P**aste to host | Inserts the contents of the clipboard into the document at the point indicated by the cursor or highlighted text or object. The result is that the information is also sent to the other host, as if the data had been typed in from the keyboard. |

The View menu

Tool Bar	If selected, the tool bar is displayed. If not, it is hidden.
Status Bar	If selected, the status bar is displayed. If not, it is hidden.
Font	This command activates a dialogue box where the display font can be changed.
Sna**p**	If selected, the window will adjust itself to the size needed by the font to display the normal screen. To reduce the display window, adjust the display font size and then execute the **Snap** command. The window will 'snap' to the new size.

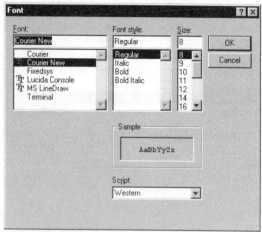

The Fonts dialogue box

The Call menu

Connect

This will make the connection as defined by the currently open file or from information added or changed within the connect dialogue box. This appears as a result of this command. If no information is available e.g. a phone number is missing, then a different box is displayed requesting the missing information, prior to the expected one.

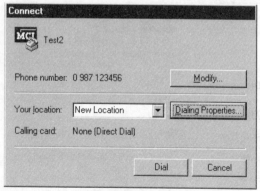

The phone number can be changed by clicking on the correct button. The location can also be changed and this is used by TAPI to add codes if the location differs from the default. For example, you can set up a location for the home and the office. The office location would have a 9 in the properties to access an outside line. Instead of changing the number when dialling in from home, the location is changed and the number converted as needed. By using this approach, telephone numbers can remain consistent and the application rather than the user makes any adjustments as required.

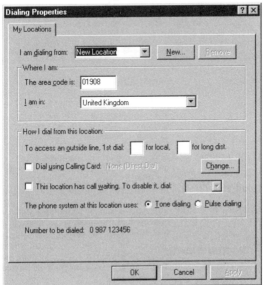

The dialling properties can also be changed by clicking the appropriate button and this also allows new locations to be created. The use of dialling properties by locations does make telephone number housekeeping easy to handle, especially if a portable is being used on the road.

Disconnect

This will disconnect the current call. It is dimmed out until a call is connected.

The Transfer menu

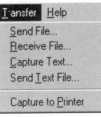

Send file

This will send a file across to the other party. This normally uses a special format to preserve the binary file structure.

Receive file This will receive a file from the other party. This normally uses a special format to preserve the binary file structure.

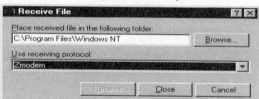

The format to be used for either the send or receive file commands is selected from the pull down menu within the dialogue box. The destination file name can also be entered using this box. The formats that are supported include the common variants of Ymodem, Zmodem, Xmodem and Kermit.

Capture text This will capture the incoming text that is displayed in the window and copy it to a text file.

Send text file This will send a file across to the other party.

Capture to Printer This will capture the incoming text that is displayed in the window and copy it to printer to get a hard copy.

The Help menu

Help Topics This accesses the on-line help facility for HyperTerminal.

About HyperTerminal
This provides information about HyperTerminal such as the revision number, licensee and so on.

The right hand button

If the right hand mouse button is clicked inside the window, a menu appears with the most commonly used commands.

Sound recorder

Unlike Windows 3.1 which usually relies on the sound card manufacturer to supply utilities that use the sound card, Windows NT supplies generic versions of the common facilities such as sound record and playback.

The Sound Recorder window

The File menu

New	Creates a new file.
Open	Opens an existing file.
Save	Saves the current file. If the file has not been saved before, a dialogue box asking for the new file name will appear.
Save As	Saves the current file with a different file name.
Properties	Reloads the previously saved recording and thus loses any changes that have been made since the file was saved.
Exit	Quit the accessory.

The Edit menu

Copy	Copies the highlighted recording to the clipboard. The document is not changed.
Paste Insert	Inserts the contents of the clipboard into the recording at the point indicated by the cursor or highlighted text or object.
Paste Mix	Mixes the contents of the clipboard into the recording at the point indicated by the cursor or highlighted text or object.
Insert file	Inserts the contents of a file into the recording at the point indicated by the cursor or highlighted text or object.
Mix with file	Mixes the contents of a file with the recording at the point indicated by the cursor or highlighted text or object.
Delete before current position	
	Deletes the sound before the cursor and removes it from the recording.
Delete after current position	
	Deletes the sound after the cursor and removes it from the recording.
Audio properties	This displays a dialogue box that defines the recording and playback volumes and audio quality.

The Effects menu

Increase volume	This command increases the record/playback volume.
Decrease volume	This command decreases the record/playback volume.
Increase speed	This increases the playback/record speed.
Decrease speed	This command decreases the record/playback speed.
Add Echo	This adds echo to the recording or playback.
Reverse	This reverses the record/playback.

The Help menu

Help Topics	This accesses the Windows NT help utility.
About Sound Recorder	
	This provides information about Sound Recorder such as the revision number, licensee and so on.

Volume control

This accessory controls the relative volumes of all the audio devices within the Windows NT system. If anyone is playing but no sound is heard, then use this utility to ensure that the volume has not been turned down low or off. The utility is self-explanatory: the vertical sliders indicate the volume level with zero at the bottom. The horizontal sliders are used to control panning between the left and right outputs and act like a balance control on a stereo hi-fi system.

If all else fails, try using the headphone socket and see if that is outputting audio. If it is not, again check it volume control and that an audio CD is in the drive. If nothing can be got from the drive, check that it will read an CD-ROM correctly. If not, then the fault is probably due to the installation and not anything with the audio links and settings. In most cases, audio faults are simple ones with volume settings and incorrect connections the prime problems.

The Volume Control window

Character map

The complete character set provided with a font is not displayed in its entirety on the keyboard. To get full access to the complete set, the more obscure characters are only available through certain key sequences or by using the direct ASCII code. Unfortunately, if you don't know what these are or alternatively what characters are supported, it is difficult to exploit them. Some applications provide this facility — Word does through its symbol command — but not all do.

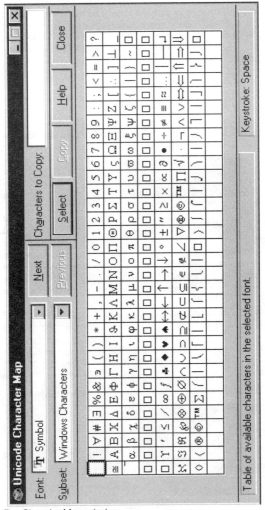

The Charcter Map window

Character Map displays the complete set of characters which can directly selected by clicking on them. The keyboard key sequence is displayed in the lower right of the dialogue box. Character sequences can be created and then copied to the clipboard for easy transfer to any application.

CD Player

With IBM PCs, the most common way of playing back the audio is through the SoundBlaster or equivalent card. The audio is routed from the three pin connector on the CD-ROM drive to a similar (but not necessarily the same!) connector on the sound card. The audio can then be played back through the speakers used with the sound card.

To get an audio CD to play, insert the disk and then call up the audio CD player utility. Windows NT is supplied with its own generic CD-ROM player which is located in the accessories program group. If no sound is heard, and the time display is active, check that the internal volume control is not turned down by opening the Volume Control accessory.

The CD Player window

The Disc menu

Edit Play List

This command allows the track list of the audio CD to be edited and thus remove unwanted tracks or change the playing order. It can also be used to reset the playing order.

Exit This command quits the accessory.

The View menu

Toolbar This option if selected, displays the toolbar.
Disc/Track info This option if selected, displays information about the CD and track playing such as the title and artist.
Status bar This option if selected, displays the status bar.

Track Time Elapsed

This displays the length of time that the current track has played for.

Track Time Remaining

This displays the length of time that the current track has left to play.

Dis̲c time Remaining

This displays the length of time that the current disc has played for.

V̲olume Control This option if selected, displays the volume control.

The Options menu

Selected o̲rder This option uses the playlist to determine the track order.

R̲andom order This option plays back the tracks in random order and is equivalent to a 'program shuffle'. If not selected, the tracks play in the standard default order.

C̲ontinuous Play This options will play back the CD-ROM, repeating the playlist if necessary until stopped. If not selected, the disc will play only once.

Intro play This option will force the play of the few second introduction to each track if the CD is provided with such an intro.

P̲references This displays a preferences dialogue box which allows the following parameters to be set:

- Large or small display fonts for the elapsed time display.
- Stop the CD playing when the accessory is closed.
- Save the current preferences on exit.
- Disable or enable those sometimes useful and sometimes annoying little yellow help messages called tool tips.
- Define the intro play length.

The Help menu

H̲elp Topics This accesses the Windows NT help utility.

A̲bout CD Player This provides information about CD Player such as the revision number, licensee and so on.

Media player

This utility is used to playback and manipulate multimedia data such as digital audio and video. The utility requires that drivers for the multimedia devices such as sound cards are installed. This is done with the **Multimedia** control panel.

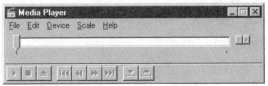

the Media Player window

The File menu

Open	Opens an existing file.
Close	Closes the current file.
Exit	Quit the accessory.

The Edit menu

Copy Object	Copies the highlighted text or object to the clipboard. The document is not changed.
Options	This command allows the user to define how to handle the end of data and other problems when manipulating multimedia data.
Selection	This allows part of the multimedia data stream to be selected.

The Device menu

Video For Windows

> This selects the driver to support Video for Windows files. It can be configured by using the **Configure** command, also in this pull down menu. The shortcut **V** is also used by the Volume Control and does not access this command although the menu indicates that it should.

CD audio	This selects the driver for CD audio files. It can be configured by using the **Configure** command, also in this pull down menu.

MIDI Sequencer

> This selects the driver for MIDI. It can be configured by using the **Configure** command, also in this pull down menu.

Sound	This selects the driver to sound (SoundBlaster) files. It can be configured by using the **Configure** command, also in this pull down menu.
Properties	This command configures the selected device.
Volume Control	This displays the volume control. This also has the same keyboard short cut as the Video for Windows option in this menu!

The Scale menu

Time	This sets the time reference for the multimedia data.
Frames	This sets the frames per second for the multimedia data.
Tracks	This is used to access MIDI tracks.

The Help menu

Help Topics	This accesses the Windows NT help utility.
About Media Player	This provides information about Media Player such as the revision number, licensee and so on.

WordPad

WordPad is a simple word processor that provides the basic ability to use different fonts, styles and effects along with simple paragraph formatting. While no where near as powerful as Word, it or to be more accurate, its format is often used to distribute 'read me' type of documents and even software manuals.

For example, all the read me files shipped with Windows NT are in this format and through its ability to read many other formats such as RTF and text, is applicable with most text documents except those from more sophisticated word processors and DTP packages.

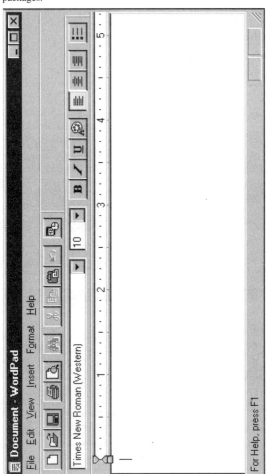

The WordPad window

The File menu

New	Creates a new file.
Open	Opens an existing file. Write will only allow a single document to be open. If you try to open another file, it will ask you if you wish to save the old one first.
Save	Saves the current file. If the file has not been saved before, a dialogue box asking for the new file name will appear.
Save As	Saves the current file with a different file name.
Print	Print the current file
Print setup	Set up print options.
Repaginate	This will repaginate the file using the current page setting.
Exit	Quit the accessory.

The Edit menu

Undo	Undoes the last operation.
Cut	Copies the highlighted text or object to the clipboard and removes it from the document.
Copy	Copies the highlighted text or object to the clipboard. The document is not changed.
Paste	Inserts the contents of the clipboard into the document at the point indicated by the cursor or highlighted text or object.
Paste Special	This is similar to the **PASTE** command but allows the data to be pasted using a special format or similar operation..
Clear	Deletes the highlighted text or and removes it from the document.
Select All	Selects all the document, ready for editting or formatting.
Find	This displays a dialogue box which requests some text and then searches the document to find it. It will find the first occurrence of the text.

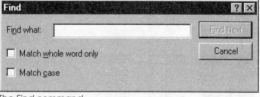

The Find command

	To find the next, use the Repeat last find command. If the document is then clicked, the cursor will be automatically placed at the text. The dialogue box will stay open if needed. It can be moved to one side and accessed by clicking on it.
Find Next	This command will repeat the find command using the previously entered text and find the next occurrence of the text.

Replace This is a variation on find where additional text is entered which is used to replace any text that matches the text in the find what box. The dialogue box will also stay open if needed. It can be moved to one side and accessed by clicking on it. Find next will go to the next occurrence. Clicking the replace button will replace the current occurrence with the new text. The replace all button will replace all occurrence within the document without prompting.

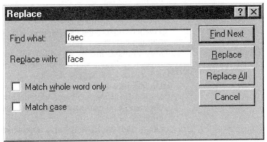

The Replace command

Links This allows access to the object linking facilities.

Object Properties This allows the properties of the highlighted object such as size to be changed.

Object This allows the properties of the highlighted object such as size to be changed.

The View menu

Toolbar If selected, the Toolbar is displayed. If not, it is hidden.

Format Bar If selected, the Format Bar is displayed. If not, it is hidden.

Ruler If selected, the Ruler s displayed. If not, it is hidden.

Status Bar If selected, the status bar is displayed. If not, it is hidden.

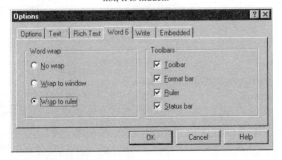

The Options dialogue box

Options

This command displays an Options dialogue box which defines the word wrap support and viewing options for each of the file formats that WordPad supports. Note that WordPad will read Word6 format files which can be very useful if the full version of Word is not available.

The Insert menu

Date and Time

This command will insert the date and time into the text at the insertion point. A dialogue box appears with a selection of many different formats and requesting that one is chosen. The date and/or time is then inserted using that format.

Object

This command inserts an object into the current text. The definition of an object is fairly loose and largely depends on the applications and hence file types that are installed on the PC, it can be a spreadsheet, a drawing, a picture, formatted text and can be taken from a file or created on the spot. A dialogue box appears requesting the object type to be selected. These are given by application name e.g. Excel spreadsheet, Paint picture and so on. Once the type has been selected, the user can fetch the object from a file or create a new one. If a file is used, the file browser opens to allow the user to select one.

If a new object is requested, then the associated application opens, a copy of the original document is copied across with a highlighted area for the new object to be created in. The application tools are then used to build the object and when complete, simply click in the document window *outside* the object. This is important to remember and will ensure that the newly created object is not lost and is transferred back. If this is done, the application will automatically close and return to WordPad with the object already in the document. The natural way of closing the document is to close the window. *Do not do this!* Do not close the object program as it will close down the application and WordPad, and lose the work that has been done! This is so easy to do by mistake.

The Format menu

Fonts

This displays a large dialogue box which allows the default font, size and style to be chosen. It even identifies the font technology and gives an example of how the text will look.

This is a common dialogue box and is found throughout many of the accessories

and other applications that offer the ability
to change a font.

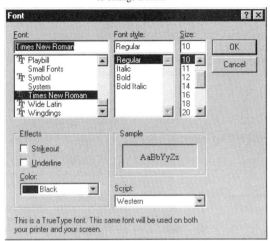

The Fonts dialogue box

<u>B</u>ullet Style   If selected, each paragraph that is either
highlighted or typed in from the keyboard
will be formatted with a bullet style i.e. a •
and a tab is inserted to create a bullet point
automatically.

> happens when you activate a package. If
> the package contains a sound or animation
> file, activating the package plays the sound
> or animation.
>
> •   happens when you activate a
>   package. If the package contains a
>   sound or animation file, activating the
>   package plays the sound or
>   animation.

<u>P</u>aragraph   This command displays a dialogue box
that allows the paragraph formatting to be
set.

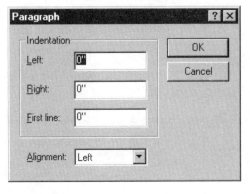

Alignment Left   This selects left alignment with a ragged edge for the paragraph e.g.

> happens when you activate a package. If the package contains a sound or animation file, activating the package plays the sound or animation.

Alignment Centred

This selects centre alignment with a ragged edge for the paragraph e.g.

> happens when you activate a package. If the package contains a sound or animation file, activating the package plays the sound or animation.

Alignment Right   This selects right alignment with a ragged edge for the paragraph e.g.

> happens when you activate a package. If the package contains a sound or animation file, activating the package plays the sound or animation.

First line   This allows a line indent to be set up. Entering a value for the left or right indents will indent the whole paragraph. Entering a value for the First line allows indented paragraphs to be created e.g.

First line set to: + 5mm

> happens when you activate a package. If the package contains a sound or animation file, activating the package plays the sound or animation.

First line set to: - 5mm

> happens when you activate a package. If the package contains a sound or animation file, activating the package plays the sound or animation. l

Tabs   This command displays a dialogue box that allows the paragraph tabs to be set. They are entered by values and it is easier to set them by clicking on the position within the ruler at the top of the window.

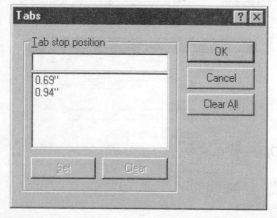

The Help menu

Help Topics	This accesses the Windows NT help utility.
About Write	This provides information about Write such as the revision number, licensee and so on.

The right hand button

If the right hand mouse button is clicked while the cursor is within the display area, a menu with the common commands is displayed as shown.

Telnet

This utility uses the network to logon to another host computer using the Telnet and TCP/IP protocols. The utility uses a terminal emulation similar to the **HyperTerminal** accessory covered previously in this chapter. To successfully connect, the remote computer's name must be entered in the **Host Name** box.

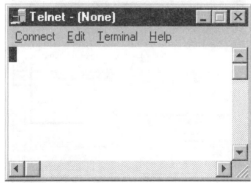

The Telenet window

Dial-up networking

This is an accessory that allows a network connection to be made over a telephone line. Its configuration is very dependent on setting up the network and as a result it is covered in Chapter 6 on Networking.

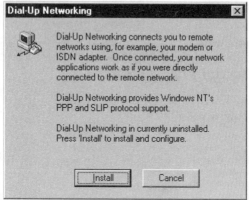

The Dial-up networking dialogue box

Phone Dialler

This is a control panel that allows the user to dial a phone number directly from the PC. It looks similar to the interface seen on a button type phone and even has a memory capability for frequently used numbers. It assumes that there is dialler hardware such as a multi-mode modem that provides the hardware capability to dial the number. Without this, the utility is of limited use.

The hardware is installed using the Telephony Control Panel via the previously mantioned TAPI interface. The accessory can also be automatically used by other applications that need to make voice calls and are TAPI compliant.

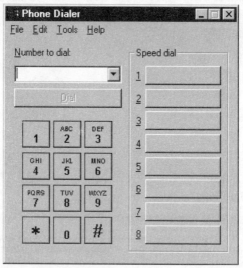

The Phone Dialler window

Imaging

This is an accessory written by Wang that allows images to be scanned in from suitable and compatible scanners. As most scanners are already shipped with suitable imaging software this utility is of limited use.

Clipbook viewer

The Clipbook viewer is a method of storing invidual objects when they are transferred to the clipboard during cut, copy or pasting operations. This accessory allows the user to transfer the current contents of the clipboard to the clipbook and vice versa. It is similar in operation with the Apple Macintosh Scrapbook. To transfer the contents of the clipboard to the clipbook, the **PASTE** command from the **File** menu. A page name will be requested and then the contents transferred. To copy a clipbook page back to the clipboard, select the required page from the clipbook window, use the copy or cut command to either copy it or cut it from the clipbook. The contents will now be transferred to the clipboard where it can be pasted into another application.

This is a useful method for keeping frequently used objects suchs as logos, addresses and other items. The accessory will allow the user to access the clipbooks on other computers within the network through the **File\\Connect** commandand the access to these remote clipbooks can be controlled and even prevented by using the Security menu commands. Successful access assumes that the user has the correct permissions to access the other computers on the network.

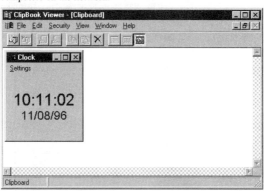

The Cipbook viewer window

Object Packager

Object Packager is a tool is used to create a package and then insert it into a document.

Its window is split into two smaller ones: the Appearance window displays the icon that will represent the package, and the Content window displays the name of the document that contains the information will be inserted.

To create a package, you copy the contents of the Appearance and Content windows, and then use the Paste command to insert the information into a document. The package appears in the document as an icon. The packaged object can now be used in other applications by inserting it into the document.

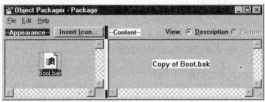

The Object Packager window

To activate a package icon, you double-click it. Depending on the contents of the package, one of two things can happen when you activate it:

If the package contains a sound or animation file, it will play.

If it contains a picture, text, or spreadsheet, the associated program with that file type will open, showing the information.

5   The Explorer

The Explorer is similar in many ways to the Program Manager in that it provides a graphical representation of the file system. Unlike the Program Manager which uses icons in the form of Program items and groups which are associated with certain programs and utilities, it displays all files including documents and data files as well as applications and system files.

The Explorer window

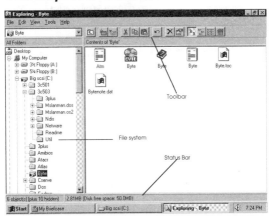

The Explorer window

The Explorer window consists essential of two halves with the left hand side used for a visual representation of the Desktop and associated files and objects. The DeskTop picture includes the contents of the My Computer and Network Neighborhood utilities and this appear at the bottom of the hierarchy.

At the bottom is the Status Bar which gives status information about commands and so on. At the top of the window below the menus is the Taskbar which contains buttons to directly access the common commands. The righthand window contains the contents of the selected item in the left hand window. In the screen shot shown, this is the contents of the folder BYTE. The size of the two windows can be adjusted by dragging the central separator to the left or right hand side as needed.

The file system icons

The left hand list represents the system through the use of icons and expand (+) and close (-) buttons to provide a hierarchical view. The diagram shows the common icons and their description. Shared files, folders, disks and other resources are depicted with small hands at the bottom of the icon. Clicking on the expand and contract buttons will contract or expand the list i.e. expand the list by showing the associated folder or disk's contents, contract the list by removing the contents from the display. The files are not deleted by contracting the list. Double clicking on an icon will also expand the list and update the right hand window with the item's contents.

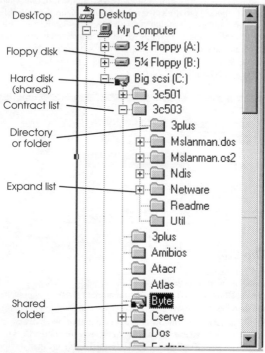

Common Explorer icons

The Explorer menus

The menus can be augmented by other commands depending on the selection made in the left hand window, so do not be surprised if the menus are slightly different. The basic commands and their actions are as follows:

The File menu

The file menu provides two types of command: the first set are a set of command-line equivalents to the normal drag and drop techniques that can be used to move files and program groups around. The second set are commands that are typically associated with commands such as delete and copy. Included in this set are the Logoff and Shutdown commands which are also available from the top Program Manager menu previously described.

Open   This will open the selected program group or file that is represented by an icon. It is the equivalent of double clicking the icon.

Create Shortcut   This command creates a shortcut of the selected file.

Delete	This displays a dialogue box which asks for the confirmation that you really do want to delete the selected icon.
Renam**e**	This activates the name box below the selected icon and allows the name to be edited or changed.
Properties	This presents the properties dialogue box and varies depending on the window and its associated application.
Close	This will close the window.

The File menu

The Edit menu

This menu is similar to the cut and paste menu found in most applications. It appears in many of the file utilities because it now supports file transfer. Files and/or directories can be cut or copied and then pasted to move files from one part of the file system to another.

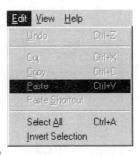

The Edit menu

Undo	Undoes the last operation.
Cut	Copies the highlighted item to the clipboard and removes it from the window.
Copy	Copies the highlighted item to the clipboard. The window is not changed.
Paste	Inserts the item stored on the clipboard into the window at a point indicated by the cursor or highlighted text or object.
Paste Shortcut	Creates a shortcut for the file that is stored on the clipboard.
Select All	Selects all the items in the window.

Invert Selection

Selects all the items that were not previously selected and de-selects those that were.

The View menu

This menu controls the appearance of the data within the window.

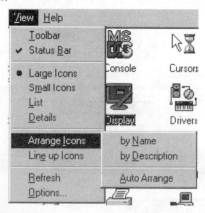

The View menu

Toolbar	This command enables the appearance of the toolbar within the window.
Status Bar	This enables the display of the status bar at the bottom of the window that gives additional information about the current activities or provides descriptions of commands and other information.
Large Icons	This changes the window display to large icons.

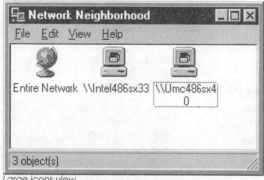

Large icons view

Small Icons	This changes the window display to small icons.

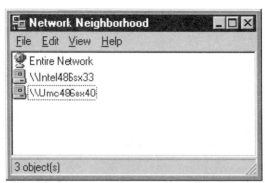

Small icons view

List

This changes the window display to a text list with small icons. To select an item, click on the name not the line.

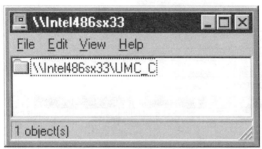

List view

Details

This changes the window display to a text list with small icons and additional information. Note that the details are not active and an item's name has to be clicked to select it. Clicking on the details associated with the item will not do anything.

Arrange Icons

This command allows the user to arrange the icons automatically without having to manually select each one and move it to its new location.

Line Up Icons

This command takes selected icons and lines them up according to the grid parameters that have been defined.

Refresh

This command updates the window contents so that any changes made to the filing system by other applications can be seen.

Options

This displays further dialogue boxes that control or restrict the amount or type of information displayed within the window. Example option dialogue boxes are shown.

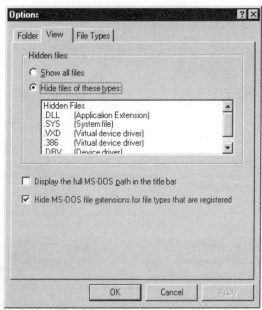

Options dialogue box

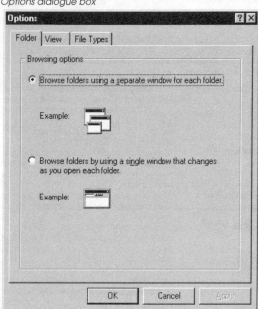

Options dialogue box

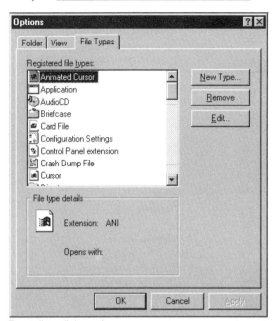

The options diologue box

The Help menu

This menu allows access to the Windows Help system for the utility.

The ToolBar

The ToolBar is a set of buttons and a drop-down menu that give access to the commonly used commands that can be accessed from the menus at the top of the window. For full details about their function refer back to the original explanation within the menu command sections. The ToolBar is optional and can be hidden by de-selecting it by using the **View** menu. There is an automatic help facility available by simply positioning the cursor over the button and waiting. After a couple of seconds, a very small window will appear explaining which command the button represents.

Drop down version of Desktop file hierarchy.

Move current position up one level.

Map Network Drive.

Disconnect Network Drive.

Cut selection to clipboard.

Copy selection to clipboard.

Paste clipboard contents.

Undo the last operation.

Delete selection.

Properties

Large Icons view

Small icons view

List

Details

6 Networking

The networking capabilities within Windows NT are very comprehensive and allow access to a large number of networks using many different network cards and interfaces. The setup and administration is relatively simple providing, as with most activities with Windows NT, the hardware and software are both compatible.

Windows NT workstations and servers

Windows NT is supplied in two versions known as Windows NT Workstation and Windows NT Server. The main difference in the packages, apart from the cost and size of the operating systems is in the support level for different network protocols. Most Windows NT installations use the Workstation version of the software which provides drivers to allow the workstation to become a client node on most networks. Also included are server drivers for Windows based networks — Windows NT, LAN Manager, Windows for Workgroups and Windows '95 — so that peer-to-peer networks can be built without the need for a dedicated server.

In addition, support is provided for accessing AppleTalk devices — mainly printers — so that networks with different computers can be created.

Windows NT Advanced Server is a more encompassing package and provides all the features that the Workstation version supports but adds the ability to be a server as well for most of the network protocols and environments. For example, AppleTalk support is expanded so that the server can provide routing functions so that AppleTalk devices such as MAC computers can be accessed by PCs on a Windows NT network.

Domains, workgroups, computers and users

A PC is accessed on a Windows NT network using its address which consists of several parts:

Domain	This is a collection of PCs and resources that are associated with a Windows NT server. Domain membership can only be usually changed if the software is re-installed.
Workgroup	This is a collection of PCs and resources that are associated with a Windows NT server. Membership can easily be changed.
Computer Name	This is the name assigned to each PC within the domain or workgroup. Its name should be unique and not be the same as any other computer.
User	This is the name who is currently logged onto the PC. For printers and disk drives that do not use the FAT (MS-DOS) filing

system, there is a special user called the **Owner** that owns the resource.

Groups

These are sets of users that have or need common privileges. If a user joins a group, the group's permissions are passed over to the user. This makes the administrator's job of controlling a system much simpler.

One of the problems that users often face with the addressing convention is confusion over domain and workgroup. This is made worse by the fact that not only do they appear to do the same job in defining sub-groups within the overall network, but are also mutually exclusive.

Workgroups and domains do essentially perform the same job in defining the sub-groups within all the overall network. This definition does not prevent other PCs or resources from outside the domain or workgroup from being accessed — it doesn't — but is does present the contents of the workgroup or domain as default.

Workgroups are sufficient within peer-to-peer networks where there is no dedicated server running the Advanced Server version of Windows NT. In this example, keeping the domain name blank will automatically place all the users and workgroups in the same domain, with workgroups differentiating the users and PCs and collecting them together.

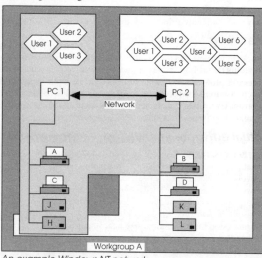

An example Windows NT network

Domains are used more in systems with a central server — usually running Windows NT Advanced Server — where parts of the network can be separated into different domains. With the server's ability to route data and resource access from one part of the network to another, it is useful to divide the network not only based on groups of PCs and users but by the network protocol or the type of physical network such as twisted pair or thin coax Ethernet, Token Ring and so on. This division is ideal for domains.

While Windows NT Workstation has some support for domains, it is largely dependent on workgroups. The administration tools that are provided are enhanced within the Advanced Server version to provide better support for domains.

In the example shown, there is a single workgroup which comprises two PCs called PC1 and PC2. Each has two printers and two hard disks and a number of users. With PC1, disk H is declared shareable within the workgroup and is accessible by users on PC2. With PC2, the printer B is shareable and is accessible by others within workgroup i.e. the three users associated with PC1. Although there is a single workgroup with two PCs connected to make the workgroup, their individual resources are can either be local or available to the network. In this example, drive H could be used to provide access to data and files by both PC1 and PC2 users. Printer B could be an expensive colour laser printer which needs to be shared while the other printers are provided locally for convenience. There are many combinations that can be defined.

Installing Windows NT, Windows '95 and WFW3.11 support

The first job to do with network support is to install the network card and software. This is normally done by the administrator — other users will not have the correct permissions to do this.

Installing the hardware

Most network installations use Ethernet and with most cards providing a range of cabling options e.g. twisted pair, thick and thin coax, it is relatively easy to install the network hardware. When installing the hardware, take note of the I/O address and interrupt level that the card will use. This is required during the installation process.

Initial software installation with the wizard

If the software has not been installed during the initial installation of the system software, then it must be done before the network will work. If the Network control panel is opened and the network software has not been previously installed, it will start an installation procedure automatically. It will first ask if you want to install the software. Click the **yes** button to continue, the **no** button to stop the installation. The next stages in the installation are handled by a network wizard.

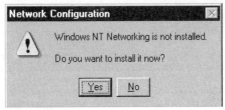

Installation dialogue

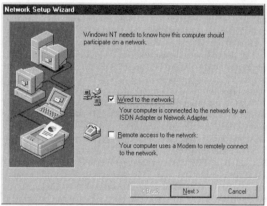

Choosing a wired or remote link

The wizard performs the installation in stages and it is possible to go back and change previous settings using the **Back** button. When the requested operation is completed, press the **Next** key to proceed to the next stage.

The first selection is to select the network link. There can be two types: wired using Ethernet, Token Ring or other network cabling and software protocol or a remote link that uses a modem to dial into the network. The wired option is the standard network link that is used in fixed installations. The remote access requires a modem at both ends and is useful for users that travel and need to access the system from remote locations. This option is setup in a similar way to the wired communication except that additional information is needed for the modem links.

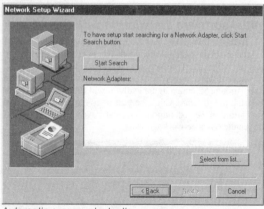

Automatic or manual selection

At this point, the wizard searches the system for network cards. This can be done automatically, where the system detects any cards by itself, or manually where the wizard is told which card is present by selecting from a list. If the automatic search does not find any boards, it reverts to the manual method where the board is identified from a list.

Once the first card has been detected, its type is displayed and at this point, the installer has several options: the first is to continue, the second is to look for other cards — Windows NT does allow multiple network cards to be used — while the third is to override the automatic search and manually define the card's identity.

Selecting the adapter card

If the adapter card's hardware settings are needed, a dialogue box will appear requesting them. It is important to get them right becuase if they are incorrect the network will fail. If the Interrupt level is wrong but the I/O address is right, the network may come up but hang when any attempt to use it is made.

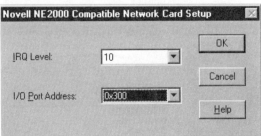

Network adapter hardware settings

The next stage is to define which network protocols the system needs. The protocols are the software components that transfer data across the network and their choice depends on the network operating system software that is needed. Most network hardware is capable of supporting multiple protocols simultaneously, and thus support many different types of connections. By default, the wizard will install the three shown in the screenshot.

Selecting the network protocol

There are three network options that are displayed and these should be considered as the three main network protocols: Windows NT supports many more but these are installed by clicking on the **Select from list** button.

The three choices are:

NW Link IPX/SPX   This is for connection to Novell Netware networks.

NetBUEI   This is the choice for connection to other Windows NT, Windows '95 and Windows for Workgroups. LAN Manager installations will also use this option.

TCP/IP   This is for access to TCP/IP networks such as those used in UNIX environments and is necessary for support of FTP and other similar utilities.

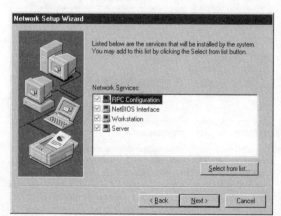

Selecting the network services

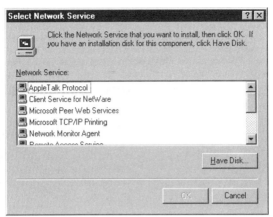

Additional services list

The next stage displays the services that will use the protocols. The Workstation service allows the computer to access shared disks and printers. The Server service allows the system to provide shared access to disks and printers. NetBIOS interface support is for legacy applications. The RPC configuration is for remote procedure call support. These are the default services. Again, additional ones can be installed by clicking on the **Select from list** button.

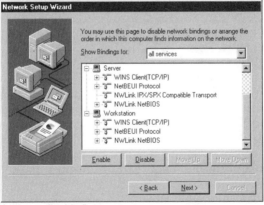

Setting up the bindings

Bindings displays the various software components such as drivers, protocols and services that are associated with a particular network card. These relationships or bindings are important if there are multiple network cards handling different protocols and networks. The bindings dialogue box also allows individual components to be enabled or disabled by selecting them and pressing the appropriate button. The items can be expanded by double clicking or clicking on the + box alongside the item. The priority of the bindings can be changed by dragging items into different order or positions if a protocol needs to run on a specific network adapter and so on. Alternatively, items can be selected and the **Move up** and **Move down** button used to move it. For most systems this can be left alone.

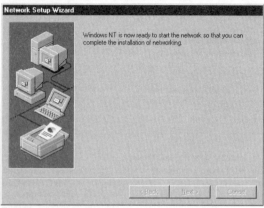

The Wizard completion window

When the wizard has finished, the network will be started so that the rest of the installation can be completed. This includes setting up the computer's name and workgroup.

Computer network details

With this information, the network can become fully functional providing the system is restarted. A dialogue box will appear requesting this is done. It is not essential that this is done immediately but networking will not become available until it is.

Normal installation

If a network has already been installed, then any changes to it are made directly through the Network control panel. As before the administrator is the user with the correct permissions to do this.

The Network control panel conisists of five sub-panels which allow all aspects of the network to be configured. They are not in the same order as the wizard uses and any changes are made in whatever order is needed.

Identification sub-panel

The identification sub-panel is where the information that identifies the computer and its user to others on the network. The first step is to identify the computer by entering its name and workgroup information. The **Change** button is used to show another dialogue box which allows the computer name and its domain or workgroup to be changed. For Windows based systems i.e. Windows NT, Windows '95 and Windows for Workgroups 3.11, the workgroup is used.

The domain is used primarily with TCP/IP based networks where the domain is an alternative grouping to the workgroup. If the domain is selected, the rest of the panel is available to set up a computer account in the domain for the computer.

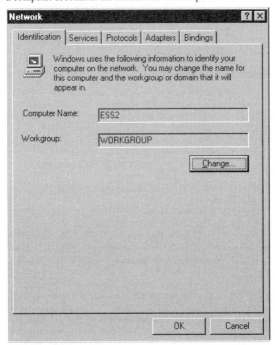

The Identification sub-panel

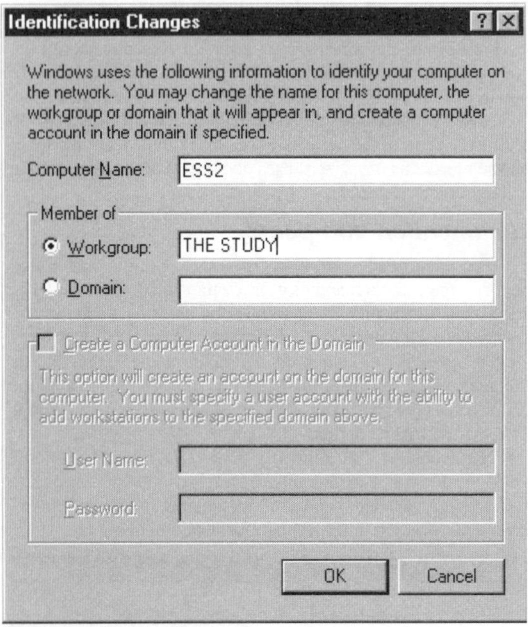

Identification Changes ? ✕

Windows uses the following information to identify your computer on the network. You may change the name for this computer, the workgroup or domain that it will appear in, and create a computer account in the domain if specified.

Computer **N**ame: ESS2

─ Member of ─────────────────────────

● **W**orkgroup: THE STUDY

○ **D**omain:

☐ Create a Computer Account in the Domain ─────

This option will create an account on the domain for this computer. You must specify a user account with the ability to add workstations to the specified domain above.

User Name:

Password:

OK   Cancel

Changing the identification

Adapters sub-panel

This sub-panel is used to install, configure and remove network hardware adapters. The screen shot shows an empty box and thus the only operation allowed is to add an adapter. The process is manual and does not support automatic detection unlike the wizard used during the initial installation. To install a card, click on the **Add** button to display a list of adapters. Choose one from this list or alternatively use the **Have Disk** button to get the system to search a floppy for other adapters. This allows a supplier to ship a floppy with the driver without having to change or upgrade Windows NT.

Once the first card has been detected, its type is displayed and at this point, the installer has several options: the first is to continue, the second is to look for other cards — Windows NT does allow multiple network cards to be used — while the third is to override the automatic search and manually define the card's identity.

Once the card has been defined, there is an opportunity to define the card's parameters such as interrupt level and I/O address. This is done by double clicking on the card in the list or selecting it and using the **Properties** button. This will display a dialogue box and is specific to the card type: some cards are configurable by software while others use hardware such as jumpers and switches. It is therefore important to have the card set up for the same parameters as supplied at this point, and to ensure there is no conflict with other hardware. For example, the I/O address and interrupt level may have been set to x320 and 12 respectively.

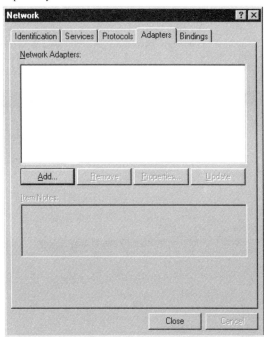

The Adapters sub-panel

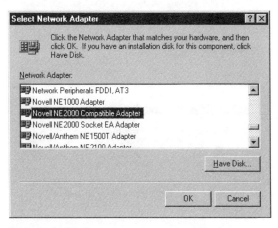

The adapter list

This is an incorrect specification because interrupt 12 is used by the floppy disk controller on a PC and thus causes a problem with the floppy disk drive. The interesting point with Windows NT is that it will usually recognise such conflicts and come back with an error message. With this example, the interrupt level was changed to 11 to resolve the conflict.

There can be other information needed beyond the expected I/O address and interrupt level. With motherboards that support multiple buses such as ISA and PCI, the system can request information about where the adapter card is located i.e. which bus and even which number in the case of multiple PCI buses.

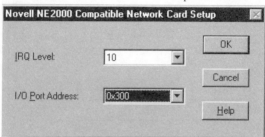

The Setup dialogue box

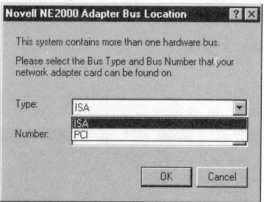

The bus location dialogue box

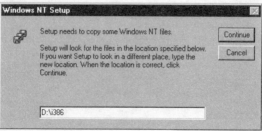

The Path dialogue box

During the procedure, there may be a request to tell the installation program where the network software is to be transferred from. This is normally the original installation CD-ROM or floppy disk drive. If the files are on a CD-ROM, change the path name to that of the CD-ROM drive and the directory where the files are located. And yes, it is a good idea to work out where this is before you start! For an Intel based system, the directory is usually /i386. For PowerPC systems, the path is \PPC. Fortunately with the multitasking support within Windows NT, using the ALT-TAB trick can get you back to the Desktop without having to answer the dialogue box or getting an annoying error beep. Once in the Desktop, the Explorer or My Computer can be used to find out and/or confirm the path name. Using ALT-TAB again can return you to the control panel.

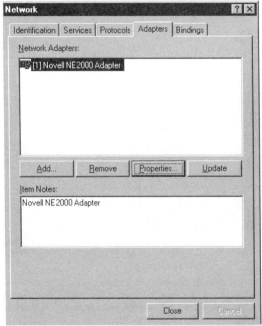

The Adapter sub-panel with installed card

Protocols sub-panel

This sub-panel defines and configures which network protocols the system needs. The protocols are the software components that transfer data across the network and their choice depends on the network operating system software that is needed. Most network hardware is capable of supporting multiple protocols simultaneously, and thus support many different types of connections. The existing protocols can be configured — although not all of them allow this — by double clicking on the protocol in the list or selecting it and using the **Properties** button. This will display a dialogue box and its contents i.e. the configuration parameters are specific to the protocol. The two common protocols that can be configured are TCP/IP and IPS/SPX Compatible transport. TCP/IP configuration is where addresses and other information is stored while the IPX/SPX configuration is where the Ethernet frame type is defined.

Choosing a network protocol

There are three network options are shown in the screenshot and these should be considered as the three main network protocols: Windows NT supports many more but these are installed in a slightly different way.

The three choices are:

NW Link IPX/SPX   This is for connection to Novell Netware networks.

NetBUEI   This is the choice for connection to other Windows NT, Windows '95 and Windows for Workgroups. LAN Manager installations will also use this option.

TCP/IP   This is for access to TCP/IP networks such as those used in UNIX environments and is necessary for support of FTP and other similar utilities.

Services sub-panel

The sub-panel displays the services that will use the protocols. The Computer Browser is used by the Network Neighborhood utility to map and display the services i.e. shared disks and printers that can be accessed across the network. The Workstation service allows the computer to access shared disks and printers. The Server service allows the system to provide shared access to disks and printers. NetBIOS interface support is for legacy applications. The RPC configuration is for remote procedure call support. These are the default services. Again, additional ones can be installed by clicking on the **Select from list** button.

The services can be configured either by double clicking an entry in the list or by highlighting it and using the **Properties** button. Most of the services do not allow any configuration. One exception from the standard set is the NetBIOS interface which allows the lana number to be changed for the various network routes within the system. The Update button allows the selected item to be updated and is used if new drivers are released.

The services sub-panel

Bindings sub-panel

This sub-panel lists the hardware and software components that have been installed and allows other components to be installed and current components to be removed or configured. Selecting a hardware or software component will enable the four buttons at the bottom of the sub-panel.

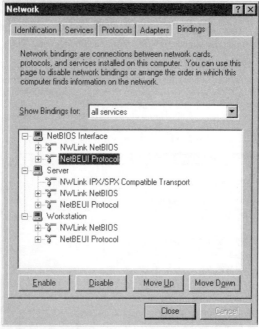

The Bindings sub-panel

It displays the various software components such as drivers, protocols and services that are associated with a particular network card. These relationships or bindings are important if there are multiple network cards handling different protocols and networks. The bindings dialogue box also allows individual components to be enabled or disabled by selecting them and pressing the appropriate button. The items can be expanded by double clicking or clicking on the + box alongside the item. The priority of the bindings can be changed by dragging items into different order or positions if a protocol needs to run on a specific network adapter and so on. Alternatively, items can be selected and the **Move up** and **Move down** button used to move it. For most systems this can be left alone.

Some components are fussy about the order in which they are deleted and will ask for other components to be removed first. If all the components are removed, then networking is completely disabled and opening the Network control panel will start the initial installation process.

Connecting to another computer

With the network hardware and software all installed, and the computer re-started, it is now possible to connect to other PCs on the network and access data on their disks and use their printers.

Using the Network Neighborhood

The easiest way to access a network drive, file or printer is through the Network Neighbourhood utility which is available on the Desktop. This is a pre configured version of the Explorer but allows shared disks to be opened directly without having to use connect commands and map the shared disk as a local drive and so on.

To open a shared disk or folder, click on the computer name to open another window with its shared resources within it. Choose the disk, folder or file and then double click on the appropriate entry. A window will open with the contents displayed as if it was connected to the local system. To transfer files, simply drag and drop them to or from the window as needed.

When accessing shared resources in this way, the first access will check the shared resource permissions and see if they match the current user. At this point there may be a request for a password. Alternatively, a message may be returned saying that access is denied. If this is unexpected, a common cause is a conflict between permissions: the local permissions given for a folder or file are overridden by those of a folder or disk drive that is higher up the file system hierarchy.

Using the Windows NT Explorer

The Window NT Explorer has a similar capability and by moving down to the bottom of the left hand display, the Network Neighborhood will be shown. This can be expanded and any network drives accessed as previously described in this section. In all honesty, this facility is ideal for transferring files and folders from one user to another. For a more permanent access — similar to that offered by previous versions of Windows NT — there are two commands under the **Tools** menu to connect and disconnect network drives.

Connecting to network disk drives

To access a network drive i.e. a drive that has been declared shareable by its owner or administrator, **Explorer** or **My Computer** is used. With the manager open, pull down the **File** menu and select the **Map Network Drive** command.

This command will display a dialogue box with a newly created logical drive letter that will be used to reference the drive and both a textual and graphical display of the drives that are available for sharing on the network.

The **Drive** list allows the network drive to be connected as any other drive by pulling down the list and making a selection. By default, it selects the first available drive letter from the list so that the existing local and network drives can still be accessed. The list will contain letters for all the total number of drives that can be connected and even allows no drive letter to be specified. This will connect the machines together without accessing the drive.

The **Path** list describes the path name of the selected drive. Note that the list starts with \\ to indicate that it is a network path name. It then uses the normal backslash delimiter. It remembers previous connections which can be selected from the drop down menu.

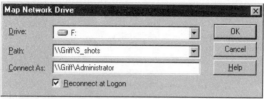

The Map Network Drive dialogue box

The **Connect As** box allows a user name to be specified. If the drive that you want to connect to is only available to certain users, then an authorised user name can be entered into the box. If the user name is password protected, this will be asked for. This mechanism permits free access throughout the system irrespective of which computer or user is being used, providing you know the correct user names and passwords. For example, if a user was logged in as a guest user on one computer and needed to access data on another using his own account name, then the drive would be selected from the display and the user's account name entered in this box.

The **Reconnect at logon** option will remember the network drive for future sessions and will automatically try and connect to the drive when the user next logs onto the current computer. If the network drive is not available — its computer could be switched off, disconnected and so on — a dialogue box will appear saying that re-connection is not possible and allowing the user to turn off the re-connection option.

Clicking the OK button will then add the network drive to the list of drives within the **Explorer**. With this complete, the drive and its contents can be accessed in the same way that a local drive is used.

Disconnecting from network drives

To disconnect a network drive from the computer, pull down the **Disk** menu and select the **Disconnect Network Drive** to access the appropriate dialogue box.

The box will display all the connected network drives — even those that have been connected without any drive letters — and all that is needed is to select the drive and click the OK button. The cancel button will stop the process without disconnecting any drives.

If the network drive has files open i.e. an application is using the data on the drive or one or more of the drive's applications are being used, a warning message appears stating that it could be dangerous to disconnect the drive without shutting down all the applications and closing any open files stored on the drive. The option is provided to carry on with the disconnect, but at your own risk! If a drive is disconnected with files still open, the data can be lost or corrupted.

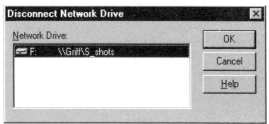

Disconnect Network Drive

Making files and folders shareable

It is possible for any Windows NT Workstation, Advanced Server, Windows '95 or Windows for Workgroups to declare a disk, directory or file to be shareable across the network. To do this for a file or folder in the right hand window involves selecting the resource within the **Explorer** or **My Computer** and then using the **Sharing** command from the **File** pull down menu. Completing all the information in the resultant dialogue boxes makes the resource appear as a network drive and thus allow network users to access it, as if it was connected to their local machine.

For a hard disk, file or folder selected in the left hand hierarchical display, the principle is the same but the the **Properties** command from the **File** pull down menu is used instead.

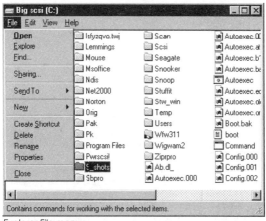

Explorer File menu

The selection can be done in a number of ways: the easiest is to simply select the disk, file or directory by clicking on the nested tree or disk icon within the display list. An alternative method for drives is to pull down the **File** menu and click on the **Find** command. This will let the user search for a complete or partial name to select the drive or folder.

With the resources selected, pull down the **File** menu once again and select the **Sharing/Properties** command as appropriate. This displays a new dialogue box which allows the sharing declaration to be set up correctly. This looks like a control panel with two sub-panels but is not. The first sub-panel called General, displays information about the resource to be made shareable, such as the size and location within the file system, the number of files and so on. The second sub-panel entitled Sharing is where the networking is set up. There is a check box at the top that enables or disables file sharing for the particular resource. This must be set to **Shared As** to allow the other parameters within the sub-panel to be changed. If set to **Not Shared**, the resource remains local to the system.

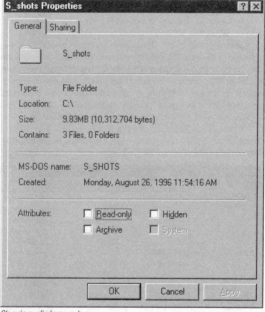

Sharing dialogue box

When sharing a hard disk, the dialogue presents an extra sub-panel called Tools which allows the hard disk to be backed up, checked or de-fragmented before being made accesible.

Share Name is where the name that is used to identify the drive is defined. In the example of how to connect to a drive, the drive was identified by a name S_shots. That name would have been entered in this box during its sharing setup. In this case the name S-shots has been used (the folder contains the screen shots used to illustrate this book). Its share name can be anything and does not have to be the same as the original name. With non-FAT(MS-DOS) file systems, the shared name can be break the FAT convention of 8+3 characters and can be upto 32 characters in length. However, if a MS-DOS system tries to share the resource, it may not see all 32 characters and truncate the name. This can be confusing if there are several long named resources with the same 11 characters. A warning message can be displayed at this point by the system

Comment is a box that is used to add any comments such as information about the resource or when it was made shareable. Anything can be put in here. A description of the contents is a very good idea.

The **User Limit** defines the number of network users that can access the network drive at any one time. It is used to limit the amount or processing that the local computer will consume in providing the data to the network. The smaller the number, the less impact that the network connection has on the local computer. The larger the number, the greater access that users on the network can have to the network drive. As expected, the value that is used is very much a trade off. Most people will start with a large value — in this case the maximum possible — and if necessary reduce the value if the load becomes too great.

The **Permissions** button will cause another dialogue box to be shown that allows the access permissions to be set up. These permissions control the access to the shared resource and effectively control who and how they can use the resource.

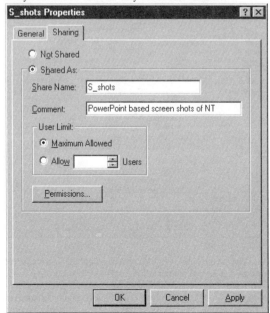

New share box

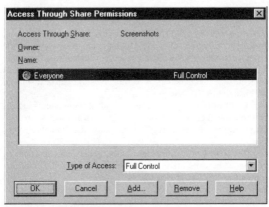

Permissions dialogue box

The box displays the access permissions for the network device — in this case S_shots. The **Owner** is often not displayed with FAT (MS-DOS) compatible drives or shared directories. The fact that nothing is there is not a problem.

Group only list

The central window shows a list of groups that can access the resource. The selected name can be removed by clicking on the **Remove** button. The **Add** button allows new users and/or groups to be added. This displays another dialogue box with the names of different groups. This dialogue box is a little confusing because when the **Show Users** button is effectively a one shot button.

When it is clicked, the list changes by adding the users to the top window. The button becomes dimmed out and there is no way back to the original list.

My understanding is that when the list is first displayed, only groups that are available are shown. When the **Show Users** button is clicked, the available users are added to the list which now includes both users and groups by name. As stated before, once the **Show Users** button is clicked, there is not a way to remove users from the list and this can be a little disconcerting to say the least.

For a highlighted name, it is possible by clicking the **Members** button to see all the members that form that group. By clicking the **Add** button, the selected name is transferred to the bottom **Add Names** list and in this way a complete list of all the required names and groups can be built up. For added names, it is possible to change their **Type of access** via the list below the drop down menu.

Group and user list

The **Search** button displays another dialogue box where it is possible to search for an user or group within parts or all of the network. The results of the search are automatically shown in the bottom display box. If these are then selected, they can be added to the list by clicking the **Add** button. By the way, the resultant dialogue box is called Find Account and not Search!

After adding or removing users and groups, the system will return to the main box containing the users and groups and the type of access that they can have. If the name entry is selected then its permissions can be changed by selecting the appropriate **Type of Access** from the pull down menu.

Four access levels are supported:

No access   Where all members of the group are barred from accessing the network drive.

Read   Where all members of the group can read the network drive but not write or change anything.

Change   Where all members of the group can read and write to the network drive.

Full control   Where all members of the group are can do anything — read, write delete, re-name and so on.

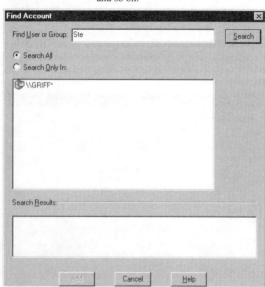

The Find account dialogue box

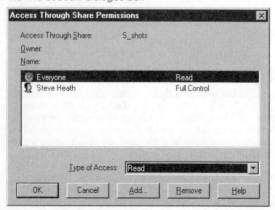

Access permissions box (ii)

The updated Access permissions dialogue box is shown with the 'Everybody' group permissions changed to read and the addition of the user 'Steve Heath' with full control. All that remains to be done is to close this and the other boxes by clicking the OK button to return to the Sharing panel. The **Apply** command can be used to update the system with the changes.

Multiple shares to the same resource

The Sharing panel through its New Share button allows the same resource to be made available to the network under several descriptions or shares. This allows different categories of access to be set up. One share could be restricted to administrators only and this is reflected in the share name e.g. Admin only.

While it is possible to have different levels of access for users and groups using the single share panel, the access becomes either all or nothing. To disable access to a group or user involves delving into the configuration and removing the user or group. Similarly restoring the access involves the same operation. By splitting the access into different shares, it is possible to simply disable a user through disabling the share. Enabling is a similar process. The disadvantage is when the resource has to be completely removed from the network and here, each share has to be disabled in turn.

Recognising shared resources

Pwrscsi!   S_shots

Shared resources can be recognised through the change in their icon. A helping hand appears at the bottom of the icon to indicate that it is shared. This does not imply that the user has the correct permissions to access the resource, but that it is available across the network.

Stopping sharing

Stopping sharing is a simpler process than enabling it in the first place. First select the shared resource (file, folder or disk) whose sharing is to be disabled. Pull down the **File** menu and select the **Sharing** command. This displays the standard Sharing panel with its two sub-panels. It will open with the Sharing sub-panel active. To disable sharing click the Not Shared radio style button at the top. If the resource is shared using multiple shares, select the next share name from the drop down menu and repeat the operation.

Be carfeul when doing this. You will typically need to be the administrator unless you have been given similar privileges. If there are remote users sharing the resource, then a dialogue box will appear saying that there are remote users still connected. It will request a time delay value — usually 10 minutes — and then use this to broadcast a message across the network to all shared users stating that the resource will be disconnected in x minutes where x is the time delay. The delay can be set to 0 where the disconnection is instantaneous. This is quick but runs the risk of corrupting all the files that the remote users were accessing. This can be extremely unpopular. This is also a good reason for getting remote users to regularly save their work, just in case this happens.

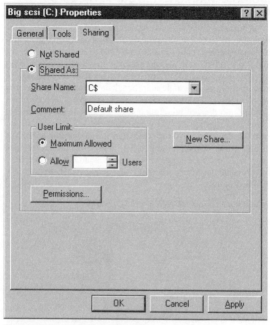

Sharing dialogue box — sharing currently enabled

Multiple permissions

Where a resource is shared, its permissions can be overridden by other permissions associated with other devices higher up in the file system organisation. For example, if a folder is declared read only for everyone and it contains a folder whose permission if full control, the sub-folder permissions will be that of the higher level folder e.g. read only. This can catch you out when the system says you have permission but the message access denied is returned. The solution is to change the higher level folder permissions, and if necessary, modify the other resources to have their own permission.

Installing AppleTalk support

One really useful feature provided by Windows NT is the ability to access AppleTalk device such as printers using an Ethernet based networks. In a mixed PC environment where it is necessary to use both IBM PCs and Apple Macs, the ability to at least share and access a printer is a real advantage. Although many AppleTalk printers support serial and parallel ports, the ability to simply attach the Windows NT computer to the network and use existing cabling is a lot easier. In addition, each Windows NT workstation can access the printer without having to go through a specific computer and placing additional workload on it.

The installation procedure that is used is similar to adding any other protocol or network service such as NFS support and so on. Although this example is for AppleTalk, the general procedure is simililar for other network components.

The installation procedure is not very complex. The first stage is to make sure that the Windows NT computer can link via Ethernet to the network. If there are other Windows NT workstations on the network then this is no problem — simply set up a network between them. If there is only one workstation, use a diagnostic program that captures Ethernet packages and check that the traffic on the MAC network can be seen. If this is visible, then the hardware should be configured correctly. The next stage is to open up the **Network** control panel and install the AppleTalk software. The procedure takes two installations: for basic printer support, only the AppleTalk protocol is necessary and must be installed. For file sharing, the AppleTalk service must be installed in addition to the protocol. The AppleTalk service is available as part of the Windows NT Server release.

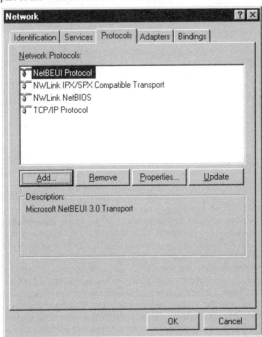

Network control panel

With the Protocols sub-panel open, click the **Add Software** button to start the procedure. This will display a second window with a list of additional protocols. AppleTalk is normally the first entry. The **Have Disk** button allows other protocols to be accessed direct from an installation disk. Either double click the entry or select it and click the **OK** button. The directory path name for the software will then be asked for and this should now be entered.

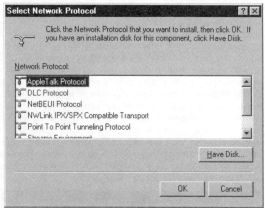

The Network Protocol additions list

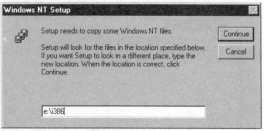

Directory path dialogue box

All that now remains to be done is to click the OK button to start the file transfer and driver installation. Like many driver installations, it is likely that a message will appear stating that the network environment has changed and that the system will need to be re-started for the changes to take effect. As part of this process, all the bindings will be updated and in some cases, the system may request some additional configuration information. For an AppleTalk installation, this is normally restricted to confirming which adapter card is used and the default AppleTalk zone that the system should attach to. AppleTalk divides its networks into sections called zones. Most installations where all the Apple MACs and printers are connected to the same network cabling consist of a single zone and this is why in most cases, the default zone can be left blank..

This request appears as a properties panel . In most cases, it can be left as it is and the **OK** button simply clicked to close the window.

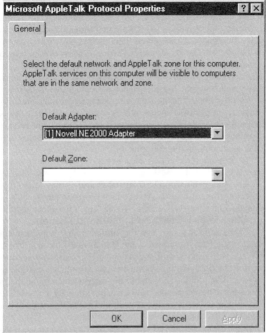

AppleTalk properties

7 Control panels

The Control panels program group is essentially the area where access to the system is controlled. It is similar to that found within Windows 3.1 but has more components and many of the facilities that Windows 3.1 configures through the Windows setup control panel are given their own control panel within Windows NT. The Windows NT version 4 follows this trend and the number of control panels has increased dramatically. In addition some panels that were previously independent entities, have been brought together under a single panel with many different options. The style has also changed: with the previous versions, the Control Panels would have a single window with lots of configuration information crammed into the space. The version 4 panels are more hierarchically based and use tabs to select sets of related configuration information.

Accessing the control panels is via the **Start** button in the TaskBar. Select the **Setting** command and this will display another sub-menu with the **Control Panel** sitting at the top. Selecting this will then open the control panel window which will contain all the panels that are available. The full path name from the **Start** button is **Start\\Settings\\Control Panels**.

The control panels and the administration tools actually modify the Registry which is the Windows NT version of the SYSTEM.INI and other files that contain the configuration information that the operating system uses. As a result, it is possible to bypass these utilities and modify the Registry directly although this is not to be recommended as it can be extremely dangerous to the system and its integrity. Play around in the Registry at your own risk! It is far safer to use the control panels.

Windows NT control panels

Windows 3.1 control panels

Accessibility options

This control panel that allows the system to be configured for those with a disability which can impact their ability to use a standard system. The panel has four sub-panels that can be configured for such use. Example changes include using on-screen visual warnings instead of system sounds and to create sticky keys where the need to press multiple keys simultaneously is removed.

Through the General panel it is possible to set a time delay that disables the options after the keyboard has been idle for a certain time period. This is useful when sharing the system.

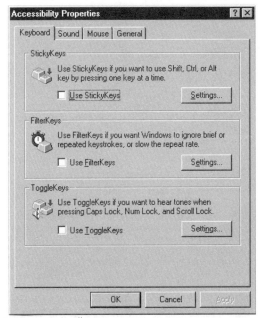

The Keyboard options

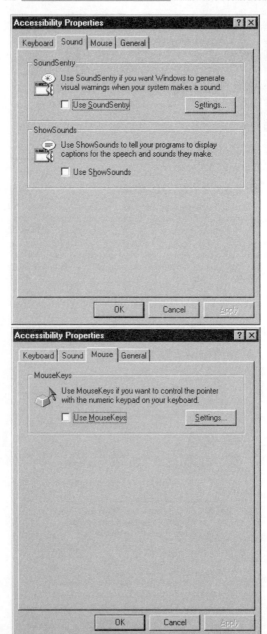

The Sound and Mouse sub-panels

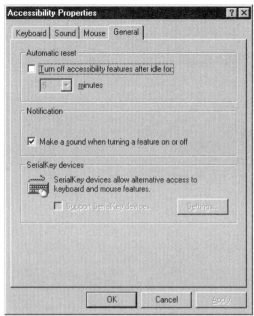

The General options

The settings for this and the other control panels that define the user interface are stored for each user. By creating different users with the administrator's tools, it allows different users to share the computer but with the Accessibility Properties either configured differently or turned off.

Add/remove Program Properties

This control panel is designed for the automatic installation and removal of software in the system. It has two sub-panels: one for installing application software and a second for installing additional system software. In the first case, it is an installation utility that allows software suppliers to automate this process but it does require the software to adhere to the rules and methodology. Not all applications do this — especially older ones — but as new versions appear, the usefulness of this panel will increase. In the case of the system software installation, this is where additional software is installed such as games, communication software and so on. The **Have Disk** button allows additional software to be installed from another disk, again providing it adheres to the standard.

The System sub-panel shows a list of components with a tick box by the side of each entry. By double clicking on a list entry or by highlighting it and clicking the **Details** button, the list is expanded to allow a finer level of choice. Ticking the associated box will install the component, clearing the box will remove it.

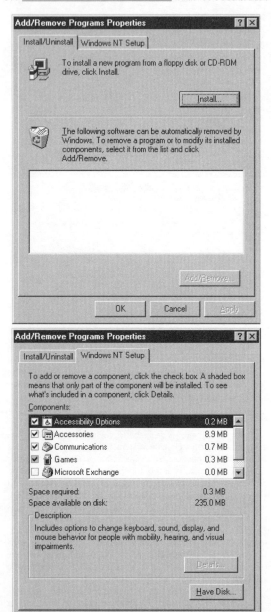

The Add/Remove sub-panels

A gray box indicates that not all the components within that group are being installed. Please note that not all the software that the system needs is installed in this way. Device drivers for sound cards, tape streamers and network cards for example are installed using their own control panels. This panel is primarily concerned with the higher levels of software upto and including applications.

Console Window Properties

This control panel defines the appearance of the Console Window which is the official name for the MS-DOS utility which allows Windows NT to run MS-DOS programs. It has four sub-panels which define the screen size, font size and type and colours.

The first panel also allows the user to specify if and how the command history is supported. This is the ability that appeared in the later versions of MS-DOS to remember and edit commands through the use of the cursor keys. It has proved immensely popular because it saves re-typing a complete command line if a syntax error was included. The user can also specify whether the window will take the full screen or simply appear in a window and thus allow itself to be re-sized and minimised to an icon or Taskbar tab entry. With a large size screen(>800 by 600) which is common, the window option is often the best choice.

The remaining three panels define the layout, fonts and colours that the utility will use.

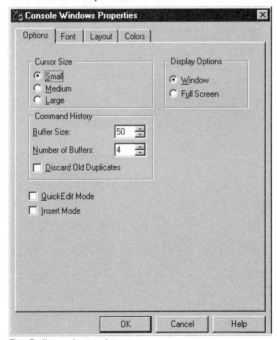

The Options sub-panel

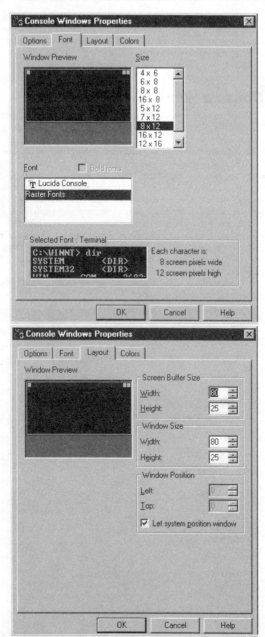

The Font and Layout sub-panels

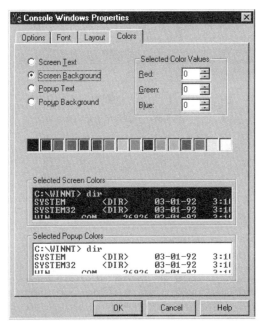

The Colors sub-panel

Fonts

This control panel is used to install, remove and configure the installed fonts that are available within the system. Unlike its predecessors that provided an alphabetical list of fonts, each font type is shown as a file and the control panel looks like a folder or directory. As an aid to help identify them, each font can display a text sample of the selected font by opening the file. This can be printed out to keep as a printed type reference. With a large number of fonts within a system, this allows a font to be chosen based on the finished printed versions instead of deciding either by name or trial and error. It is interesting to note that many fonts have an individual font for each differing style such as bold, italic, bold-italic and so on. This is often done to provide a better quality font with less work as opposed to taking the generic plain text font and enhancing it to support the different styles.

To remove a font, select it from the list and use the **Delete** command from the **File** menu. To add a font, use the **Install New Font** command from the **File** menu and follow the instructions. A dialogue box will appear asking for the location of the font that will be installed.

The **View** menu allows the fonts to be seen as icons or as a list and also can group similar fonts together, and even hide the bold and italic versions for greater clarity. The simarlarity option is useful in that it allows a font to be chosen and then categorises all the other fonts in terms of their simarlarity. This makes life a lot easier when maintaining a consistent font style that needs different variants for haedings and so on.

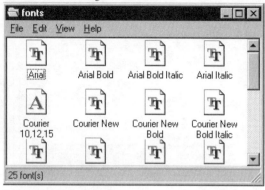

The Fonts control panel

The Truetype (TT) icon identifies Truetype fonts. This may be important if the printer that is being used only supports these type of fonts or is more effective with Truetype. PostScript fonts are designated with the A icon. In most cases today, printers can use either font and this is not a problem.

Ports

The ports control panel is one that is quite popular and appears to come up with many different programs and control panels. It essentially allows the serial ports to configured correctly and is used by the HyperTerminal accessory, the Printers control panel and so on. It consists of three dialogue boxes: the first displays the ports that are available and by selecting one, it can be deleted or set up by clicking on the appropriate button. Additional ports can be set up as well clicking on the add button.

Changing the port configuration goes across users i.e. the users do not have their own configuration stored in the same way that a user's colour scheme is specific to that user. However, changing the configuration will require in most instances for Windows NT to be re-started and a dialogue box will appear with both don't restart now and a restart now buttons. For mere users, the restart now button can be clicked but sometimes nothing happens. If the administrator changes the settings, the restart now button will work, the system will shutdown and restart. The reason is that the port may be used by devices such as printers that are being shared by others on a network and therefore a user may not be allowed to change the settings. The system has to be restarted so that the driver software can use the new configuration and that in itself can also be disastrous to anyone who is connected to the system via a network.

In practice, this means that the administrator should be the only one to change the ports settings even though a user can change settings such as the baud rate and so on without the need to re-start the system. There is a further restriction placed on the serial port hardware and that concerns sharing hardware interrupts. With a normal PC running Windows 3.1, it is possible to install four serial ports and allow them to share the two interrupts that are normally allocated to serial ports between the four.

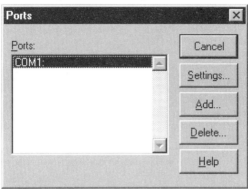

The Ports dialogue box

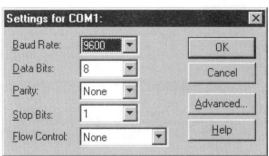

The Settings dialogue box

Advanced Settings for COM1:		
COM Port Number:	1 ▼	OK
Base I/O Port Address:	Default ▼	Cancel
Interrupt Request Line (IRQ):		Help
	Default ▼	
☐ FIFO Enabled		

The Advanced Settings dialogue box

Interrupt 4 is used for COM1 and COM3 while interrupt 3 is used for COM2 and COM4. Providing COM1 and COM3 are not used at the same time or to be more accurate needed at the same

time, the interrupt can be shared. This is also true for COM2 and
COM4. While this will work with Windows 3.1, the interrupt
sharing will not work for Windows NT 3.x but does appear to
work for version 4. I was surprised but pleased, when I upgraded
my system and found that I could access COM3 with no problem.

Although serial ports COM3 and COM4 can be created and
configured to share interrupts with COM1 and COM2, they may
not be available for use and an attempt may result in an error
message such as ''file COM4 is not available'. The solution to this
problem is to use serial ports that can be hardware configured to
use other interrupt levels and allocate a different hardware interrupt to each new port. This then allows the ports to be created and
configured with unique interrupt levels and the problem is solved.
This is fine, but most serial cards do not have this facility and apart
from cutting tracks and re-soldering the interrupt signal to a
different interrupt level pin, there is nothing else that can be done
except to replace the card.

The other different phenomenon is that serial ports that are
allocated or being used by other devices are not listed in the ports
dialogue box. For example, if a serial mouse is using port COM2,
then this port would not be available for use.

Internet

This control panel is used to set which server on the network
is to be used to provide a connection to the Internet. This server is
known as a proxy server and all Internet requests are routed
through it across the network and out to the net if this control panel
has been used to configure the service.

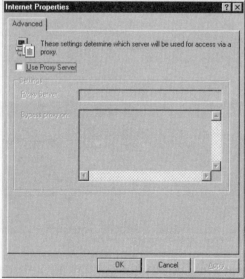

The Internet Properties Control Panel

Mouse

This control panel consists of four sub-panels and provides control over the mouse and pointers (cursors in Windows NT 3.x terms). It is one of the new panels that incorporates several of the control panels found in previous versions. Please note that the **Apply** button must be used to apply any changes to the settings.

The Buttons sub-panel allows the user to set the speed and of a double click and allows a user to swap over the left and right buttons if needed. This can be useful for left-handed users or right handed users that wish to use the numeric keypad and thus use the mouse with their other hand. Clicking on the appropriate check box will not only swap the buttons over with the right hand button becoming the one that activates menus and so on, but the L and R within the mouse drawn in the middle of the dialogue box will also switch over.

The slider bar is used to set the double click speed and this setting can be tested by double clicking on the box in the righthand window, alongside the slider. If the double click is fast enough, the box springs open.

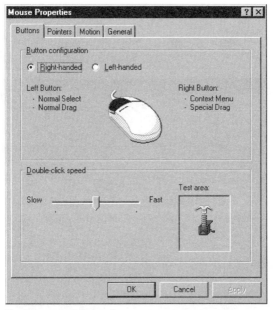

The Mouse control panel

The Pointers sub-panel allows the cursors for arrows, waiting and so on can be changed. Windows NT uses the Windows 3.1 defaults for its set of cursors e.g. the hour glass, outline arrow and so on, but also supports colourful dinosaurs and other options.

The motion sub-panel is where the tracking speed of the mouse can be changed.

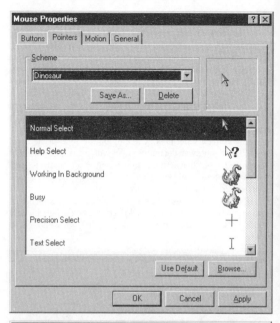

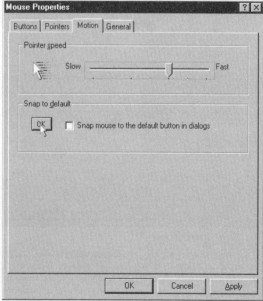

The Pointera and Motion sub-panels

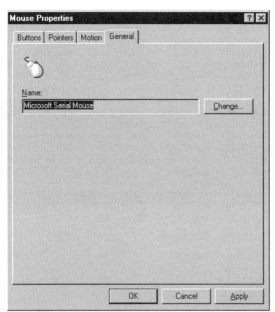

The General sub-panel

The final sub-panel allows the driver to be changed for the mouse. The mouse type is automatically detected on installation and the appropriate driver chosen. Some mice can support several different types and this panel gives an opportunity to force a driver to be used instead of the currently installed driver. Again, like the display settings, the mouse settings are remembered for each user and are thus any changes are specific to that user and no one else.

It is not uncommon for three button mice to appear as two button mice with the middle button unused. This appears to be a feature of Windows NT and should not be considered as a fault.

Keyboard

This control panel sets up the keyboard and consists of three sub-panels. The first one defines the auto repeat characteristics. The top slider sets the delay between pressing the key down and starting the key repeat. The slider below it determines the rate at which the key repeats. The bottom box is a test area which can be used to try out the settings. Pressing a key will enter that character into the box. Holding it down will then cause the key to be repeated. When the key repeats, the charter is repeatedly entered in the box. In this way, the settings can be easily checked. In addition the cursor blink rate can also be changed by the slider at the bottom.

The next sub-panel defines the locale or language layout for the keyboard. It allows the language and thus the layout to be set up so that pressing the Z key will actually generate a Z on the screen. While the most common change is in the area of £,# and other similar characters, the changes can also affect letters such as Y and Z. On a French keyboard this are swapped over, for example. If a the screen is not displaying the correct keys, then check this sub-panel.

It is possible to support multiple locales with one locale designated as the default. Special key sequences can be defined to switch between them and an indicator can be enabled within the TaskBar to indicate which locale is being used. The advantage that this offers is that it allows a keyboard to be configured as French when using a word processor so that the additional French characters such as ç and ê can be directly accessed from the keyboard. This can be a very useful feature in Europe with its multitude of languages.

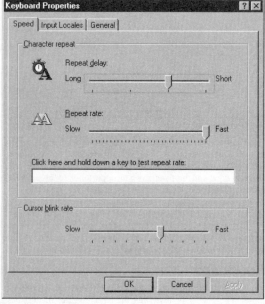

The Keyboard control panel

The final sub-panel is used to define the keyboard type in terms of the system (AT or XT) and the number of keys that it may have. Throughout the development of the PC, there have been different keyboard arrangements with differing numbers of function keys and cursor keys. While the PC/AT 101/102 enhanced keyboard has become a default, there are other smaller keyboards available. This sub-panel is used to define which keyboard is used. If the wrong definition is used, then the majority of keys will work fine but often the important keys such as : and \ will have moved. The result is that pressing the key will result in a different character appearing!

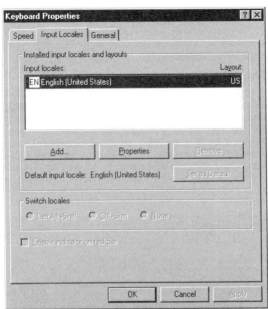

The Locales control panel

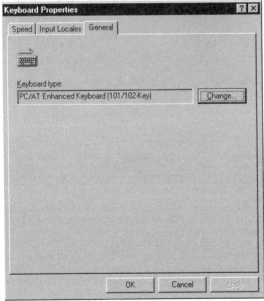

The General Control panel

Printers

The printers control panel is quite complex and as a result, it has been given a complete chapter to itself. For more details please refer to Chapter 8.

Regional

This control panel allows the nationality of the system to be set up. It is here that the country, language layout and other formats can be configured. These will normally be set up during installation but they can be changed using this control panel. Some changes will result in the system prompting for special files and/or disks that contain the special configuration files. If some keys on the keyboard cause different characters to appear on the screen — # instead of £ for example — then the problem is usually caused by an incorrect keyboard layout and this is where it can be corrected.

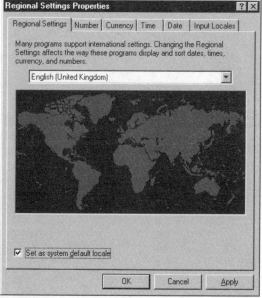

The Regional control panel

The control panel has six sub-panels. The first one sets up the local region and this then by default selects standard formats for numbers, currency, date and time and so on. This can be changed by accessing the appropriate sub-panel and making an appropriate choice. The final sub-panel defines the locale or language layout for the keyboard. It allows the language and thus the layout to be set up so that pressing the Z key will actually generate a Z on the screen. For more details, see the previous section on the Keyboard control panel.

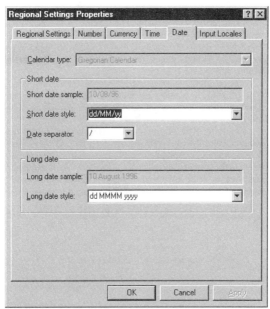

The Regional date control panel

SCSI Adapters

This control panel is used to configure all the drivers used to access hard disks, CD-ROMs and other devices attached via the SCSI bus. In reality, the term SCSI is loosely applied because it also includes access to the IDE interfaces as well. It consists of two sub-panels.

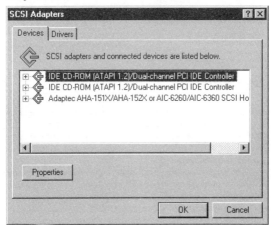

The Devices sub-panel

The Devices sub-panel displays the devices that are recognised and the list can be expanded by clicking on the + box or line item. This will reveal the devices or drives that are connected. More detailed information about an item within this window can be obtained by highlighting it and then clicking the **Properties** button.

The resulting window has three sub-panels which gives the configuration information. The most useful is the Resources sub-panel which will indicate which I/O address and interrupts it will use.

Returning to the original control panel window, the Devices sub-panel displays a list of drivers and gives the ability to add new drivers or remove existing ones. This is used if new hardware is added to the system to install the appropriate driver. If the existing hardware is being used and a different driver or upgrade is required, the existing driver is removed using this sub-panel.

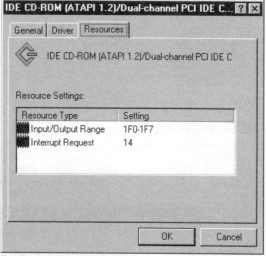

The Properties window

System

This is a special control panel that defines the system configuration such as the startup options, virtual memory and recovery procedures. The control panel is split into two parts: the first allows control over the system as a whole and is not user specific. The second part allows the user to configure variables specifically for the user and no one else.

The Startup/Shutdown sub-panel allows the startup messages to be defined: the preferred operating system can be defined along with the list time out value. Typically there is a 30 second delay before the system will boot up the preferred operating system and this allows enough time to select an alternative operating system such as MS-DOS to be selected instead.

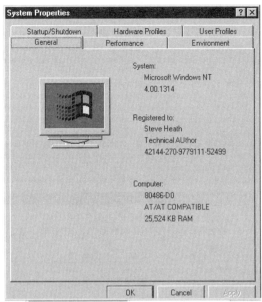

The System control panel

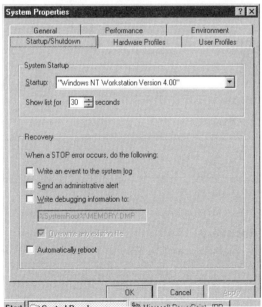

The Startup/Shutdown control panel

By setting the time-out to zero, the system can be forced to boot Windows NT every time and thus force the use of a floppy disk to boot anything else such as MS-DOS. The default 30 second time out option is probably the best to use because it at least gives some options, in case something goes wrong and you need to run MS-DOS.

The system environment variables are displayed in the Environment sub-panel and these can also be changed by clicking on the variable which will cause the variable name and value to be transferred to the two smaller boxes below. The details can be changed and the new version confirmed by clicking the set button. Alternatively the variable can be deleted by clicking the delete button. The box below shows the user environment variables and these are changed in a similar way. This can be used to create special paths for a user and set up variables for applications to use.

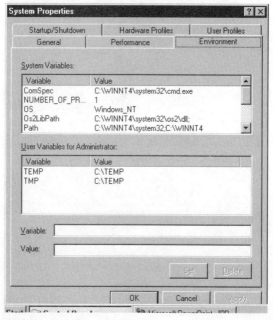

The Environment control panel

Recovery

The Startup/Shutdown sub-panel also controls the systems response to a STOP error. Due to the protection environments that applications run in, a fatal error will rarely bring down the system and thus the system can provide several different responses (unlike Windows 3.1 which would inevitably cause you to press CONTROL-ALT-DELETE or the reset button).

The choices that Windows NT offer are:

- Write an event entry to the system log, thus making a record of what happened and when.

- Send an alert message to the administrator so that he can sort out the problem.

- Write debugging information about the error to a special file.

- Re-boot the system (known as the Windows 3.1 compatibility mode!)

Any combination of these choices can be made by checking the appropriate entries in the control panel.

Virtual memory

The Performance panel controls the virtual memory capability of Windows NT and allows the swap files and their location to be configured. Windows NT supports up to 16 swap files simultaneously with one paging (swap) file per drive. This means that large paging files can be distributed across a set of smaller drives. In the configuration shown, one paging file is setup on driveC with a file size of 36 Mbytes.

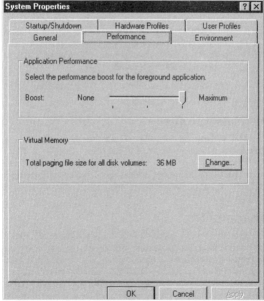

The Performance control panel

The paging files can vary in size and it is possible to receive messages saying that the swap file is full although the size specified has not been exceeded. This anomaly is due to other files being saved to the disk and taking up disk space so that the paging file cannot be expanded. The control panel will also recommend a paging file size for the amount of physical memory in the system. This recommendation can be ignored but if set too small, the system will rapidly run out of memory and limit the number and/ or size of applications that can be run. If set too large, the system will be able to support large numbers of applications or a few very big ones, but system performance will be lost because of all the paging to and from disk that the system will have to do. The recommendations presented in this panel are a reasonable compromise of giving sufficient memory against system performance. The system from which this screen shot was taken had 20 Mbytes or RAM installed in it.

Tasking

The Performance control panel also allows the user to customise the level of response that is needed for foreground and background tasks.

Three options are provided:

- Best foreground response where any background tasks get little or no processing time. This is the default setting and is probably the best for users that use one application and want the best performance.

- Better foreground response where background tasks get some processing time. This is a better setting for users that do multiple tasks e.g. spreadsheet calculations can be performed in the background while a word processor is running in the foreground.

- The democratic setting where foreground and background tasks get similar processing times.

Hardware profiles

This sub-panel is used to configure different hardware configurations which can be used at the startup sequence. These configurations can be changed to enable/disable networking and so on. These configurations can be copied and edited as needed. By default, the system will automatically create an original configuration.

User profiles

This sub-panel is similar to the hardware one except that it stores the settings for a particular user. Again, they can be copied and edited as needed to create new entries. The profile can be used as a roaming entity which is used automatically when that user logs onto any machine within the network. What happens is that the profile is fetched from the home machine and is used by the local system.

This is useful on large networks where there are virtual users who can use any available machine and therefore are likely to use many different systems and do not wish to maintain profiles on all of them. However, this choice is available if needed.

Telephony

This control panel is new to version 4 and is used to install telephony devices and obtain calling information for use with TAPI compliant applications such as HyperTerminal. It consists of two sub-panels: the first allows information about the current location to be defined such as the number needed — if any — to access an outside line and so on. This information can be stored in different location profiles so that changes can be made by selecting a different location instead of changing the settings themselves.

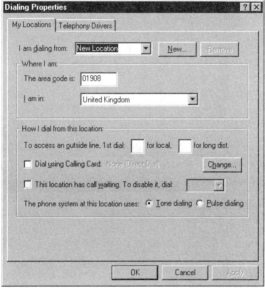

The My Location sub-panel

The second sub-panel allows devices such as modems to be installed. These are installed by double clicking on the Unimodem Service Provider. Other TAPI devices and drivers can be installed and/or removed by selecting the appropriate button.

The modem installation process can be performed automatically or manually. There is a wizard available that guides you through either process and gives you two choices: either let the system sutomatically detect the modem or alternatively, you can choose it from a list. If the modem is not on the list, it is usually possible to choose either a generic type — Hayes copmpatible for example — or one that is similar.

The automatic detection can take some time — several minutes is not uncommon — and needs the modem to be connected and switched on. Failure to do either of these operationscan cause the auto-detection to fail and the message that no modem was detected. With a built-in modem, this is less likely to happen.

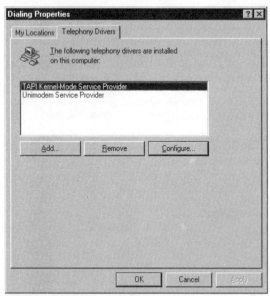

The Telephony Drivers sub-panel

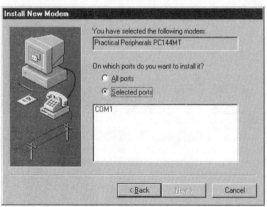

The Install New Modem wizard

This control panel is automatically invoked if no modem has been installed and a TAPI compliant application such as the HyperTerminal accessory is used. It can even be accessed from the application itself if needed.

In this way, it is possible to use a modem or other telephony device without it having to open this control panel at all! For more detailed information about the relationship between this control panel and its information and the HyperTerminal accessory, refer to the section on HyperTerminal in Chapter 4.

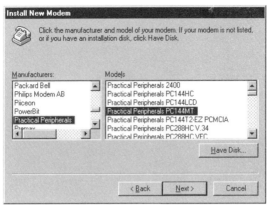

The Install New Modem list

Tape Devices

This is similar to the SCSI Adapters control panel in that it performs the installation and configuration of tape streamers primarily attached to the SCSI bus, but also including some of the IDE and Floppy based controllers as well.

The Devices sub-panel displays a list of installed devices and through the **Properties** button can allow a selected device to be configured.

The Drivers sub-panel allows drivers to be installed and/or deleted. If new hardware or a tape streamer has been added, then this panel must be used to install the appropriate driver and configure it. The installation normally requires a system restart to make the driver software and thus the tape streamer available to the system. The Backup utility, provided in the Administrator's toolkit, can access the tape streamers and backup/restore the data stored on the system, either on local disks or across the network.

The Drivers sub-panel

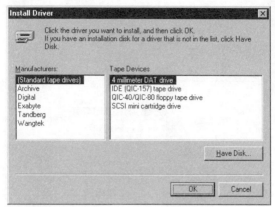

The Tape streamer list

Date and Time

This is where the system date and time is set up (this cannot be done through the clock accessory). Apart from the ability to set up the date and time, the time zone and associated daylight saving can also be chosen. Clicking on your location on the map is sufficient for the control panel to select the appropriate time zone. Alternatively, the drop down menu at the top of the sub-panel can also be used to make a more manual choice. The daylight saving option is particularly useful as it means one less clock to change twice a year — providing the programmed chage over dates are the same as set by the local government! Sometimes they are not and the the time can be an hour out.

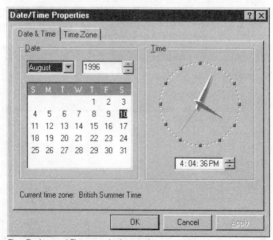

The Date and Timecontrol panel

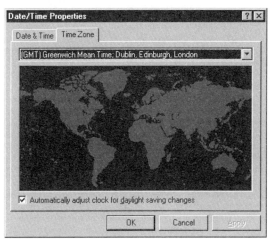

The Time zone panel

Display settings

Unlike Windows 3.1 which performs display changes through the Windows setup program and thus, requires new drivers to be added and the system restarted, Windows NT uses a special control panel and allows changes to be performed on the fly, although there are some restrictions to this.

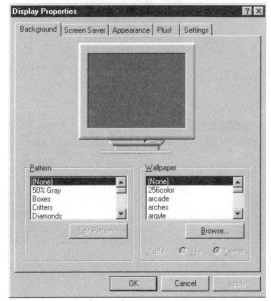

The Background sub-panel

Even so, the abiltity to change screen size and colour when required is extremely useful especially when getting screen shots for books and documentation. With version 4, it is split into several sub-panels with each one controlling some aspect of the system display.

This is where the look and feel of the desktop is set up. It is similar to that found within Windows 3.1 and allows the desktop background pattern to be defined — in the screen shot it is set to none— along with any wallpaper. The use of the ALT-TAB key used to be controlled here as well but this option is now switched on permanently with version 4. By holding the ALT key down and repeatedly pressing the TAB key, all the currently running programs and tasks are displayed one by one. To go to the program, the ALT key is released when the program name appears in the dialogue box.

The Screen Saver sub-menu is where the user can select and configure one of the many screen savers than those available within Windows 3.1 including the now infamous 3D pipework screen saver that draws a myriad of pipes in three dimensions. This does involve a lot of floating point processing and even on a fast 80486SX can be very slow due to the lack of an on-chip floating point unit.

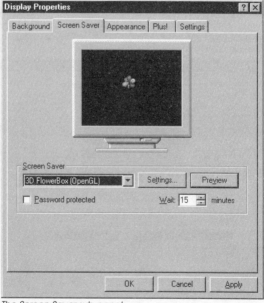

The Screen Saver sub-panel

The Appearance sub-panel allows the user to set the colour scheme used by the user interface. The colours can either be selected by a scheme or by directly accessing the colour palette and effectively creating your own scheme. Once the correct scheme has been selected or created, clicking the Apply button will confirm the choice and change the colour scheme. The scheme is defined for the current user and if a different user logs on, their choice will remain unaltered.

The Appearance sub-panel

The monitor at the top changes its display as the area is changed through the top right slider. The colour depth can be changed via the top left menu. The monitor refresh rate and the choice of size for the default screen fonts are also provided.

There is one word of advice I can give with colour schemes: if the scheme involves white text on a black background — a choice that many prefer — it is possible to lose Microsoft Word text or diagrams when documents are transferred from an Apple Macintosh or from another Windows system. The reason is that the text and/or drawing objects are set up to be black and thus disappear when they are shown on a black background. The solution is to set the colours up to be auto selected or white whereupon the missing objects should re-appear.

The colour scheme that is selected is specific to the user and different Windows NT users can select their own configuration. When they log on by pressing CONTROL-ALT-DELETE, Windows NT will use that configuration and not the default or previous setting.

The Plus! sub-panel is new to Windows NT and allows the icons used for the various desktop items such as the recycle bin to be changed. It also controls the full drag option. When set, windows are dragged across the screen or re-sized as complete windows and not as outlines which are filled in when the window is released. The full window is less efficient and slower but does allow the contents to be displayed at all times which can be beneficial when re-sizing. There are two new options. One will stretch a wallpaper image to fit the screen — this can distort the image and therefore not worth using. The other option smooths the edges of fonts and the final one forces the use of icons with the same colour depth as the screen i.e. all the possible colours are used.

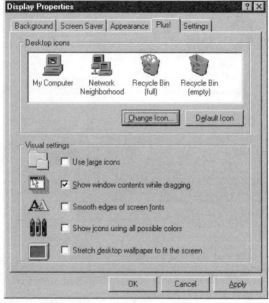

The Plus! sub-panel

The Settings sub-panel is used to adjust the screen size, its colour resolution and to change the graphics driver if necessary. Graphics drivers for Windows NT tend to incorporate many different modes and this allows the Settings sub-panel to change the settings in many cases without having to load a new driver. A new configuration can be tested by clicking the Test button. This displays a special screen for a few seconds which shows different colours, lines and text. If this is unreadable, clicking the mouse button will restore the old setting. If it is fine, then the new settings can be confirmed b clicking the OK button as normal.

The settings can be overridden when booting the system by choosing the Windows NT (VGA) option when selecting the operating system. This is will start the system in VGA mode and thus allow the user to use this control panel to reconfigure the display settings to a compatible set.

The Settings sub-panel

Server

This control panel provides information about who is sharing the file and printer resources of the computer i.e. it allows the user to see who is using the computer as a server — hence its name. The buttons at the bottom of the control panel are used to identify which aspect of network use is to be displayed i.e. which users are active, who is sharing drives over the network, which drives are in use and so on. The whole aspect of servers and networking is covered in Chapter 6.

The Server control panel

Sound

This is similar to the control panel within Windows 3.1 and allows various system events to generate a sound. This assumes that there is a suitable sound card installed in the system and its drivers have been loaded. Clicking on the speaker will play the sound. Sound configurations can be saved as schemes if needed.

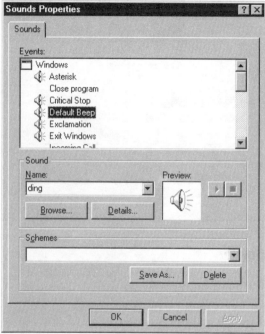

The Sound control panel

Network settings

Again, like the printer control panel, the Network settings are complex enough to warrant their own chapter. This control panel is used to identify network cards and install low-level drivers, as well as high level software to support network connections. It is possible to support several protocols over a single card and the configuration and binding of the network hardware and protocols is also controlled by this control panel. See Chapter 6 for information on this control panel and examples of how to set up a network.

Devices

This control panel displays the devices that are active in the system and their status. This panel is again intended for advanced users who need to start and stop parts of the system. By selecting a device, the buttons on the right hand side become active allowing the selected device to be started up, stopped or re-started.

Please be careful when using this control panel as stopping or disabling drivers can cause a lot of system problems unless you are sure of what you are doing.

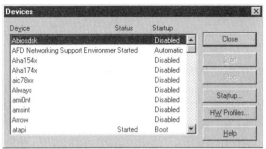

The Devices control panel

Services

This control panel displays the services that are active in the system and their status. This panel is intended for advanced users who need to start and stop parts of the system. By selecting a service, the buttons on the right hand side become active allowing the selected device to be started up, stopped, paused or re-started.

Please be careful when using this control panel as stopping or disabling services — as with devices — can cause a lot of system problems unless you are sure of what you are doing.

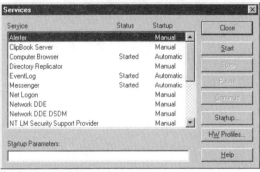

The Service control panel

UPS

This control panel is used if an uninterruptible power supply — known as a UPS — is used with the computer to supply power if the mains supply is disconnected. It can normally supply power for a limited time period and this control panel allows the communication between the UPS and the computer to be configured. Typically, they communicate using a serial port and pass signals from the UPS to the computer indicating some kind of power failure. The resulting action is set up using this control panel.

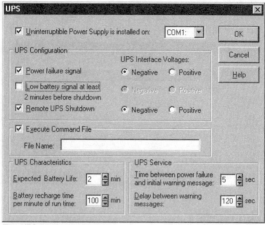

The UPS control panel

Multimedia

This control panel consists of five sub-panels and controls the configuration of the multimedia devices within the network. This control panel is new and combines several of the old control panels from previous versions such as the MIDI Mapper and Sound Mapper.

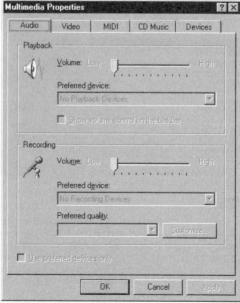

The Audio sub-panel

The Audio sub-panel determines the which device is used to playback sound files. It specifies the priority order of various drivers so that if several sound sources are played back simultaneously, the drivers will be given priority depending on these settings. In addition, it allows the user to specify which sound card is used for playback. Windows NT supports the generic SoundBlaster type cards but its sound support is limited compared with that offered by Windows 3.1.

The screen shot shows a panel with dimmed out controls. This is due to the fact that Windows NT version 4 does not install multimedia drivers by default and therefore this is the default state. To enable the controls, a driver must be installed using the Devices sub-panel.

The Video sub-panel configures the video playback that can be performed with Video for Windows. It allows the playback to be expanded to take the full screen or to retain its normal size. Playing back on a full size screen is frequently detrimental to the playback speed and picture quality. The picture quality is often degraded because the expansion is done by making the pixels occupy more space. The result is a picture where the image is blocky and grainy. With the larger amount of video data that the processor has to move, the playback speed is often reduced, further reducing the quality of the image.

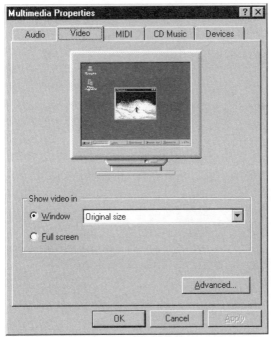

The Video sub-panel

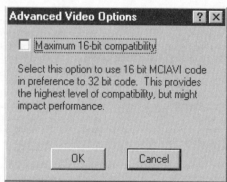

The Advanced Video Options window

The advanced settings control the use of the 16 or 32 bit MCIAVI software video codec. The original versions of Video for Windows used 16 bit code and thus this window gives an opportunity to trade the aadditional performance that the newer 32 bit versions offer for the highest level of compatibility. If playback of old video clips is a problem, this might be an option worth trying. For most uses, however, it can be left as it is.

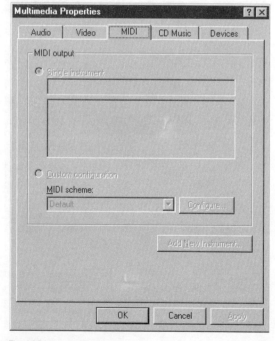

The MIDI sub-panel

The MIDI sub-panel determines the which device is used to playback MIDI files. Typically, this is routed through or mapped to the MIDI synthesiser that most sound cards have but it can also be routed through to an external MIDI controller and then onto any MIDI compatible instrument such as a keyboard or synthesiser.

The screen shot shows the default window with no active devices and the controls dimmed out. This is because it requires that MIDI drivers are installed using the Devices sub-panel, which is covered later on in this chapter.

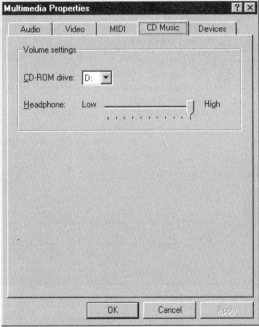

The CD Music sub-panel

The CD Music sub-panel allows the volume settings for music playback to be defined. It works with multiple CD-ROM drives which can be selected from the drop down menu. Please remember that there are other controls associated with volume and these are configured by the Volume accessory.

This control panel determines the which device is used to playback multimedia files, such as sound, video and MIDI. It specifies the priority order of various drivers so that if several sound sources are played back simultaneously, the drivers will be given priority depending on these settings. The priority is dependent on their position within the list. The priority can be changed by moving devices up and down the list by dragging them. In addition, it allows the user to specify which sound card is used for playback. Windows NT supports the generic SoundBlaster type cards but its support is limited compared with that of Windows.

The sub-panel shows a listing of multimedia types and devices and the list can be expanded by clicking on the + box or double clicking on an item. Clicking on the **Properties** button with an item clicked will display more information about that item.

The Devices sub-panel

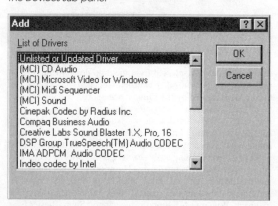

The Add window

The device properties window

This sub-panel is where drivers/devices are added. The type must be selected first and then the **Add** button is clicked. This then displays a list of drivers from which to choose. To be consistent, there should be a Have Disk button but instead one of the choices is an unlisted driver. Choosing this has the same effect — a request for the driver disk. In the screenshots shown, the type is an audio device and the list is of SoundBlaster and similar devices.

The required device is double clicked or highlighted and the **OK** button clicked. This will create an entry in the list. As part of the installation process, the device can be configured as to which hardware addresses and interrupts it uses and so on.

It may be necessary to restart the system before the drvice can be used.

8 Printing

The Printers control panel is used to control and set up the printing facilities that are offered with Windows NT. It replaces the old Print Manager found in the previous versions of Windows NT and does the smae job: the installation and control over printing within the system. It follows the normal practice for multi-tasking operating systems in offering background printing where the document to be printed is first printed to a file and then sent to the printer via the Printers control panel. The advantage to users is that an application can continue to be used even if the printer is busy with a different document. In other words the days of waiting for a document to print are gone.

This chapter goes through all the commands that are available through the Printers control panel and includes, a detailed step-by-step explanation of how to create a printer icon i.e. configure the system to recognise a printer.

Concepts

The basic concept behind the Printers control panel lies in the definition of a printer and document. A printer is as it name suggests a printer, but in the world of Windows NT, a printer is one that is either local to the computer or is available across the network. The system can support multiple printers e.g. the computer could have one on a parallel port, another on a serial port and a couple sitting on an Ethernet network if needed.

When a file is printed, it is turned into a document using the printer driver that is associated with the target printer. The target printer is selected either by default — through the Printers control panel — or can be changed by the application through an option within the application's print dialogue box. Some applications do not support this feature and in this case, the Printers control panel is used to set the default printer.

The documents — also referred to as print jobs — are queued to be sent to the printer. The Printers control panel also handles the queues and allows the queues to be re-ordered, paused and stopped. Documents can also be deleted and even printed if the current user has logged off. If the computer is shutdown before a document can be printed, it will be printed the next time the computer is started up.

The Printers control panel window

The Printers control panel is accessed via the **Start** button and the **Settings** menu as shown. To get full access and thus set up and configure a printer will normally require the Administartor, or a similar empowered user, to perform the installation and changes When opened displays a similar window to that used for the Explorer or My Computer. It will sometimes come back with a message saying that it cannot be opened. The Printers control panel relies on several background tasks to be running before it can be active. If these are not active then the message appears. It is possible on a slower machine, to try and open the Printers control panel before these tasks are running. If this type of message appears, simply wait a few seconds and try again. Another possible cause for this message is the wrong access permissions. If this is the case, then the administrator or equivalent user must set up the printer.

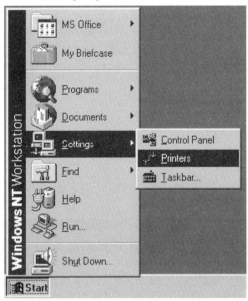

Accessing the Printers control panel

The window initially contains a single file which is the Add Printer Wizard. When a printer has been installed, its icon is added to the window and by opening this special file, the printer and document control window can be accessed. This is similar to the old Print Manager.

The Printers control panel

Installing a printer

This procedure has been made easier in Windows NT v4 by the provision of a Add Printer wizard that is located in the Printers control panel. Open this wizard by double clicking on its icon or selecting it and using the **File\\Open** command. The wizard will open and guide you through the process.

The Add Printer wizard icon

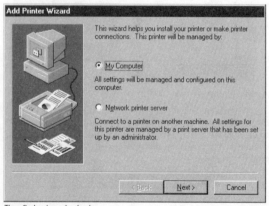

The first wizard window

Selecting a port

The first part of the installation is to select the physical port that will be used to connect to the printer. This is usually a parallel port such as LPT1 or a serial port like COM2. The available choices are shown in the next wizard panel. The required port is selected by clicking on the lefthand box alongside the appropriate entry. This will tick the box. With a selected port, it is possible to configure the communications so that the computer and printer can transfer data. The configuration window is accessed by using the **Configure Port** button. With a parallel port, the configuration parameters are limited to a timeout value. With a serial port, this is where the baud rate and associated parameters are configured. This is similar to the configuration necessary for the HyperTerminal accessory and for further information, please refer to it in Chapter 4. Needless to say, it is important that the port is correctly configured.

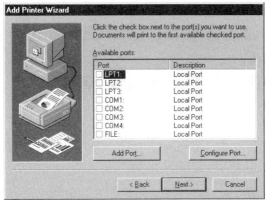

Selecting a port

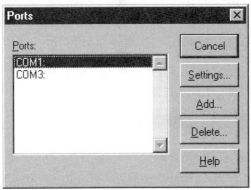

Configure port window

Connecting to an AppleTalk printer

By default, the only available ports are those that are physically part of the system. However, there are printers that have direct network connections such as AppleTalk and DECnet printers. To access these, the **Add port** button is used to bring up another window with a list of alternative ports. AppleTalk will only appear if its protocol software has been previously installed using the Network control panel. For more details about this, please refer to Chapter 6. Double clicking the entry or selecting it and clicking the **OK** button will start the system searching the

AppleTalk network that it is connect to for AppleTalk printers. The next window shows the results of its labours and depicts the printer Production Printer in its list. At this point, if no devices appear after a reasonable time, check that the printers are switched on and everything is connected to the network including the Windows NT computer.

Adding an AppleTalk port

Selecting an AppleTalk printer

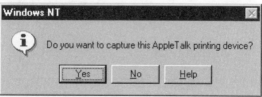

The Capture dialogue box

Select the required printer and click the OK button. The next stage is a little strange in that it will ask if you want the printer to be captured. This means that the printer is taken over by the Windows NT computer and is accessible only through this system. For Apple MAC users on the network, this can mean that printer access is now dependent on the Windows NT system and is not usually accepted as a good idea. As a result, capturing is normally disabled and the offer rejected. A non-captured printer will appear as two printers to other Apple MAC users: it will be seen under its normal stand-alone Apple name as well as its

Windows NT description. Printing can be sent to either but with
the Windows NT version, the information is sent to the Windows
NT system which then forwards it to the printer.

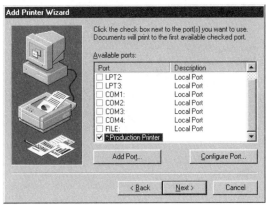

The revised port window

After completing this part of the process, the AppleTalk
printer will now appear as an option within the printer list
displayed by the wizard. It must be selected to use it before
pressing the **Next** button.

Defining the printer type

The procedure continues as normal. The next stage is to
define the printer type that is connected to the port. This is done
by making a selection from a list. With the printer type defined, a
name is then assigned to it. This name is used as the title of the
printer icon that represents the physical printer connected to the
port. It is a good idea to put some form of location or description
in the name to make locating the printer easier.

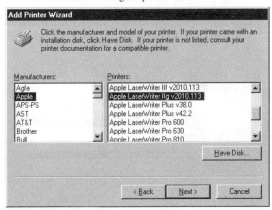

Defining the printer

Assigning a printer name

After assigning the printer's local name, the next window of the installation process is to decide if the printer is shareable across the network. If it is, then the appropriate chcek box must be selected to enable the dimmed options within it. These include, the name of the printer that will be used across the network to access it and the types of systems that will be using it. This includes different versions of Windows as well as Windows NT v4 running on non-Intel based processors. If an operating system is chosen that uses MS-DOS or MS-DOS file systems, then the printer name may have to be restricted to the normal 8+3 characters that the MS-DOS file system uses. If this is not done, non-conforming names will be truncated to the 8+3 format and this can lead to confusion where the truncation generates the same name from two or more printers. A warning message will appear if this is a possibility and request that the name is changed. This is only a recommendation and a long name can be used except that it may be truncated to give a MS-DOS compatible name.

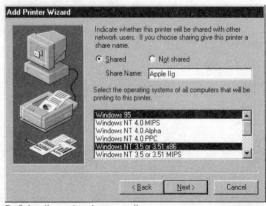

Defining the network connections

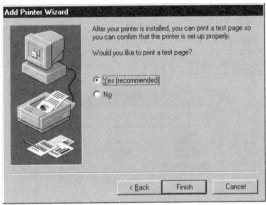

The test page window

The final part is to print a test page. This tests the connection, printer and configuration. Sometimes, the wizard will request the original installation disk(s) to retrieve a test page. Do not be surprised if this happens. Simply insert the disk and set up the directory name e.g. E:\i386 for an Intel installation from drive E. E:\PPC for a PowerPC installation from the same drive and so on.

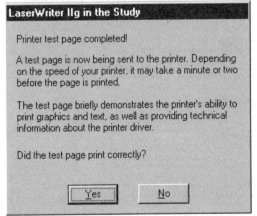

Installation complete

The last window asks for confirmation that the page printed correctly. Clicking the **Yes** button will complete the installation. Clicking the **No** button will allow the installation to be changed in case there was a mistake.

Installing multiple printers

It is possible to install multiple printers by simply repeating the process for each printer and giving each one a different name to allow it to be uniquely identified.

Configuring a printer

Once a printer is installed, it can be configured by changing its properties. This can be done by selecting the printer within the Printers control panel and using the **File\\Properties** command, or alternatively, by opening the printer and using the **File\\Properties** command from within the Printer window.

The Printers control panel

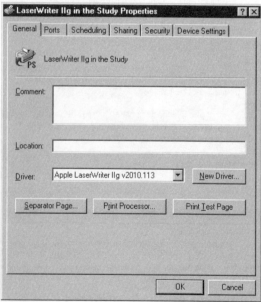

The General sub-panel

The General sub-panel is used to change the driver and or print processor that is being used with the printer. The driver is normally associated with the printer while the print processor is typically associated with the printing technology that is being used e.g. PostScript. There is also the ability to test any changes with by printing a test page. The separator file allows a file to be nominated that will be printed with each print job. This should have the user's name and contact information and is mainly to allow people to identify whose printout is which.

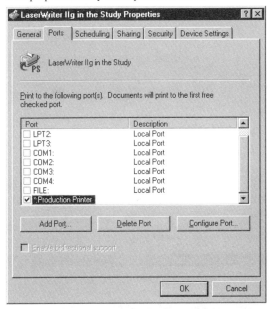

The Ports sub-panel

This is similar to the wizard window that defines and sets up the printer connection. It has the same commands and allows the physical ports such as the parallel and serial ports to be configured as well as add network based connections such as AppleTalk.

The Scheduling sub-panel is where the printers availability and other configuration data can be configured. The printer's availability can be controlled via the **Available from** settings. The printer can be made available all of the time or by setting the two times, between a certain period of the day. The priority level, the print processor and default data types can all be set here. In addition, it is possible to re-direct the print out to other ports or even a file to create a backup or produce multiple copies on multiple printers. The remaining check boxes determine the course of action when the print job is complete. Printing directly to ports is a slightly dangerous option especially if the serial port is shared between several devices. If this is the case and this option is enabled, there print job may be sent directly to the port when it is being used with a modem. The result is the modem receiving both printer data interleaved with the real data that it expects.

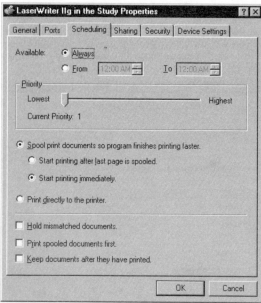

The Scheduling sub-panel

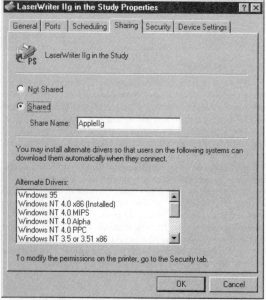

The Sharing sub-panel

The Sharing sub-panel allows the network name for the printer and the types of networked systems that will use the printer to be defined. It is essentially the same as the equivalent window presented by the installation wizard. Remember the possible restriction on the printer name with MS-DOS based systems.

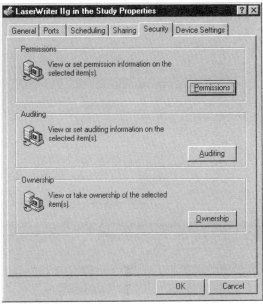

The Security sub-panel

This sub-panel sets up the security aspects of the printer i.e. printer permissions, auditing and owner. To set up the permissions, click the **Permissions** button. This will display a box which will allow users and groups to be added and for each one, set the required permissions. The permissions define the level of access i.e. what a user can do.There are four levels that can be set for groups and users:

Full control	Full unrestricted access
No access	No access to the printer
Manage documents	The ability to queue, pause and re-order documents in the print queue as well as printing.
Print	The ability to print documents with no document management ability.

To change a particular permission, select the user or group and then choose the permission from the drop down menu below it. Repeat as necessary before applying the changes — the **Apply** button — and clicking the **OK** button.

The auditing window will initially appear blank with most of the buttons dimmed. The first action that must be done is to define the users and groups that can access the printer. This is done by clicking the Add button. With a user or group installed, the auditing can be set up by clicking in the appropriate check boxes. Either a success, a failure or both can be audited for the various events shown in the panel.

The Printer permissions

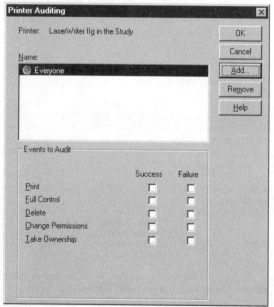

Printer auditing

This provides traceability for the network or system administrator to see who is using the printer and in which ways. The success/failure categories are useful in providing a metric concerning the system's reliability and can be used to isolate — and then address and solve — faults that the users and groups may be encountering.

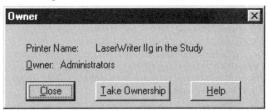

The Printer owner

The owner dialogue box allows the owner of the printer to be changed, providing the taker has the relevent permissions to do so. This can be used by a remote administrator to take over a remote printer across the network so that it can be changed or re-configured.

The Device settings sub-panel

The Device settings sub-panel allows the printer configuration to be changed by selecting a topic — usually in blue lettering enclosed by < > brackets — and changing its configuration from the small box below the main display window. This window displays the current default settings. Some of these can be overridden by the Print dialogue box that most applications use. These changes are only applical to that print job. Common changes include paper tray selection and the paper (form) size. In this example, the printer memory size is being changed. Sometimes, you can get strange messages such as 'not enough memory and you really don't want to change this' message. I've normally left it alone and everything has been fine. This was certainly the case with previous versions of Windows NT but version 4 does appear to have solved the problem.

To make the printer the default — in a large system there may be many icons representing many different physical printers and/or configurations — change the entry in the **Default** text box in the upper right of the window.

Controlling a printer

The Printer control panel is for all intents and purposes a folder and as such it has a set of commands that allow direct access into the sub-panels to change the configuration and so on. The commands are essentially to do with the configuration of the printer and related services, and not directly with documents and queues. These are handled in a separate window which is accessed by opening the printer icon. This is covered in the next section.

The File menu

The file menu provides two types of command: the first set are a set of command-line equivalents to the normal drag and drop techniques that can be used to move files and program groups around. The second set are commands that are typically associated with commands such as delete and copy. Included in this set are the commands to control the printer

Open   This will open the selected printer that is represented by an icon. It is the equivalent of double clicking the icon.

P<u>a</u>use Printing   This will pause the printer is the printer is active and re-start the printer when it is paused. A tick by the command shows that the printer is paused.

P<u>u</u>rge Print Documents
This will clear any printing that the printer has in its document or job queue.

Set as Def<u>a</u>ult   This will set the printer as the default printer for this system.

S<u>h</u>aring   This will open the sub-panel that controls the sharing of the printer by other systems on the network. This is where sharing can be enabled or disabled.

Document Defaul<u>t</u>s
This command will allow the paper size to be configured through its Page Setup sub-panel and allow the printer's complete re-configuration through its advanced sub-panel.

S<u>e</u>rver Properties   This will open the Server Properties panel which allows additional configuration of ports, paper sizes and auditing.

Create <u>S</u>hortcut   This command creates a shortcut of the selected file.

<u>D</u>elete   This displays a dialogue box which asks for the confirmation that you really do want to delete the selected icon and thus the printer.

Rena<u>m</u>e   This activates the name box below the selected icon and allows the name to be edited or changed.

<u>P</u>roperties   This presents the properties dialogue box for the printer. It is the same panel as previously explained in the preceding section on configuration.

<u>C</u>lose   This will close the window.

The Edit menu

<u>U</u>ndo   Undoes the last operation.
Cu<u>t</u>   Copies the highlighted item to the clipboard and removes it from the window. Typically dimmed and not available.
<u>C</u>opy   Copies the highlighted item to the clipboard. The window is not changed. Typically dimmed and not available.

Paste	Inserts the item stored on the clipboard into the window at a point indicated by the cursor. Typically dimmed and not available.
Select All	Selects all the items i.e. printers in the window.
Invert Selection	Selects all the items that were not previously selected and de-selects those that were.

The View menu

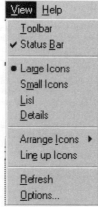

Toolbar	This command enables the appearance of the toolbar within the window.
Status Bar	This enables the display of the status bar at the bottom of the window that gives additional information about the current activities or provides descriptions of commands and other information.
Large Icons	This changes the window display to large icons.

Large icons view

S_m_all Icons   This changes the window display to small icons.

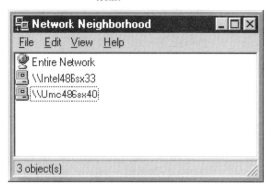

Small icons view

_L_ist   This changes the window display to a text list with small icons. To select an item, click on the name not the line.

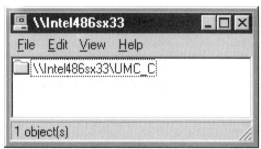

List view

_D_etails   This changes the window display to a text list with small icons and additional information. Note that the details are not active and an item's name has to be clicked to select it. Clicking on the details associated with the item will not do anything.

Arrange _I_cons   This command allows the user to arrange the icons automatically without having to manually select each one and move it to its new location.

Lin_e_ Up Icons   This command takes selected icons and lines them up according to the grid parameters that have been defined.

_R_efresh   This command updates the window contents so that any changes made to the filing system by other applications can be seen.

_O_ptions   This displays further dialogue boxes that control or restrict the amount or type of information displayed within the window.

The Help menu

This menu allows access to the Windows Help system for the utility.

Controlling a printer queue

With all the printer details and settings configured correctly the printer is ready for use. Double clicking the icon for the required printer within the Printers control panel will display the status of the printer and the number of print jobs that are waiting. This new window is where the printer and associated print jobs are controlled. This can be accessed by anyone except those with their permissions set to 'No access' or 'Print'.

Printing a document is performed via the Print command within the application. This will spool the document and it will appear in the printer window as a document. The commands available in the Printer and Document menus provide control over how it is printed. In many aspects, this window shares a lot with the previous one but it is the only one where there is access and control over individual documents.

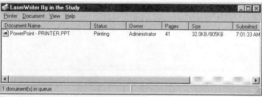

The Printers panel

The Printer menu

Install	This will access the printer installation wizard and install a printer. Typically , this command is dimmed out and not available if a printer has already been installed.
Pause Printing	This command will pause the currently selected printer so that any printing it is doing is stopped until the resume command is used.
Resume	This command will resume a paused printer so that it will continue its current printing job.
Purge Print Documents	
	This command will remove all documents that are waiting to use the selected printer.
Set as Default	This will set the printer as the default printer for this system.

S̲haring
This will open the sub-panel that controls the sharing of the printer by other systems on the network. This is where sharing can be enabled or disabled.

Document Defaul̲ts
This command will allow the paper size to be configured through its Page Setup sub-panel and allow the printer's complete re-configuration through its advanced sub-panel.

Re̲fresh
This command will update the information within the window.

P̲roperties
This command sets up all the parameters associated with the printer. This is very similar to the Create Printer command except that the printer already exists. The basic functionality is described here but for full details see the section on connecting an AppleTalk printer which goes through the process in detail. This is described in Chapter 6

C̲lose
This closes down the window but does not stop the printing. This will continue in the background.

The Document menu

This menu is greyed out until a document is selected from a printer window. It controls the document printing and allows the priority and time of printing to be changed from the default. To enable these commands, it is necessary to select a document from within the list first.

P̲ause
This will pause the printing of the current document. If the document is already printing, the computer will not send any more sate to the printer. This can be used to halt any printing while special paper is loaded.

R̲esume
This will resume the paused printing of a document.

Re̲start
This will restart the document printing from the beginning. This command should only be used if the printer is in a good known and working state. Some printers if they have the current document aborted, can lock up and fail to print any future jobs. The only solution is to reset them i.e. switch the power off and on again.

P̲roperties
This command displays detailed information about the currently selected document. It also provides the ability to change the priority of the job, a start time, a wait until time and which user should be notified that the when the printing is complete. These options are set by pulling down the appropriate lists and making a selection.

C̲ancel
This command will remove the currently selected document from the print queue. In this way the document is prevented from

printing — permenently — and its corresponding file deleted form the file system. The only way to print the document is to go back to the original application and data file.

The View menu

Status bar   This option determines if the status bar is visible or not. A tick alongside the menu entry indicates that it is visible.

The Help menu

This menu allows access to the Windows Help system for the utility.

Summary

The Printer control in version 4 is different from its predecessors. In some ways it is easier to use by virtue of its move away from a single entity to control everything towards a more modular approach. On the other hand, it can be a bit misleading when some commands are available and others are not. This does tend to make the unfamiliar user scratch one's head trying to remember 'where that document command is?'

In summary, here are the three interfaces that a user needs to remember and how to access them.

• To install a printer

Start\\Settings\\Printers\\Add Printer

• To control a printer:

Start\\Settings\\Printers\\File menu

• To control a print queue on the printer called 'Desktop':

Start\\Settings\\Printers and open the Printers folder.

Select the printer icon called 'Desktop'.

File\\Open to open the window.

Use the **Printer** and **Document** menus to control the printer and documents

9 Administrative tools

The Administrative Tools program group contains a set of utilities that allow a system administrator to perform the various administrative jobs such as creating new users and groups, enforcing the system security, backing up the system and so on. The set of tools are by default only accessible by the Administrator or a user who is a member of the Administration group. For other users, this window is hidden or not available. If needed, wider access can be granted by the administrator to other users but this should not be done without careful consideration because these utilities can damage the system irrevocably if used incorrectly!

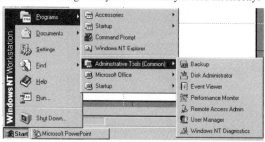

The Administrative tools window

The User Manager

The User Manager is, as its name suggests, the utility for handling users and groups and their associated rights. This utility is used to set and change passwords, define how much or how little of the system a user can access and other related activities.

Before a user can log into the system, the users must be set up using this utility. Each user is given an account which is referenced by the user name. The user is assigned rights to the various part of the system either directly or by making him a member of a group so that he inherits the group's system rights. A user can be a member of several groups if needed.

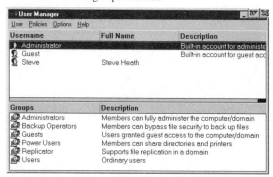

The User Manager main window

The window is split into two halves with the top half displaying the users that the system knows about and the bottom half shows the groups that have been defined for the system. A user or group can be selected by simply clicking on the appropriate entry. In the screen shot, the user 'Steve' has been selected and is highlighted by inverting the line. Double clicking the entry will display the **Properties** box and is an alternative to using the **User\\Properties** command

The User menu

This is the most used pull down menu as it provides access to the user and group configuration commands.

<u>U</u>ser	<u>P</u>olicies	<u>O</u>ptions	<u>H</u>elp

New <u>U</u>ser...
New <u>L</u>ocal Group...

<u>C</u>opy...	F8
<u>D</u>elete	Del
<u>R</u>ename...	
<u>P</u>roperties...	Enter

| E<u>x</u>it | Alt+F4 |

New <u>U</u>ser   This command will create a new user for the system. A dialogue box appears asking for information about the user and asks for the name, a description and a password for the user. The user name can be up to 20 characters long and include both upper and lower case characters, including number but excluding punctuation marks. The full name is optional but would normally contain the full name of the user and even a location. It is not used to identify the user when logging in, but simply provides a better method of recognising the user.

The New User window

The first three check buttons are self explanatory and define the initial password policy. The fourth check box will disable the account so that it cannot be used. This is a quick way of disabling the user's account without having to completely remove the user's entry and set up data. It can also be used to set up a template user which can be copied to create a new user simply by changing the name. This is quicker than performing the job from scratch.

New User\\Groups

This button will display another dialogue box which will allow the user's membership of other groups to be defined. By default a user is made a member of the Users group. To add additional memberships, the required group is selected from the right-hand list and the Add button clicked. To remove membership, the group is selected from the left-hand list and the Remove button clicked.

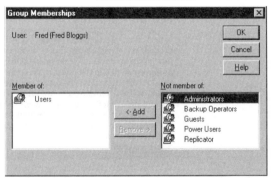

The Group Membership window

New User\\Profile

This window sets up the environment for the user and defines the home directory for the user. Typically, each user is given their own directory for the storage of their own data files. The location of this directory is normally put into the Local Path box. The Logon Script box can be filled with a path name to a script file that will be executed when the user logs on to the system. The script file is similar to the batch files found in MS-DOS and Windows 3.1. The Connect box allows the name and location of any network drives that users needs to be entered. These will then be automatically connected when the user logs on. For this facility to work, the user must have an account on the network machine using the same user name and with enough rights to access and share the drive. If this is not done, then the connection will fail. In addition, the network system should be powered up. This is an easy thing to overlook!

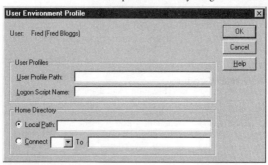

The User Environment Profile

New Local Group   This command creates new groups and is similar in operation to the **New User** command. It asks for the name of the new group and a description of the group. In the screen shot, the name is 'Windows NT production' and its description is 'Production group for book'. The members of the group are shown in the bottom box in the window. By default this box is empty and to add members, the Add button must be clicked. To remove members from the group, the user is selected by clicking on the appropriate entry in the box and the Remove button clicked.

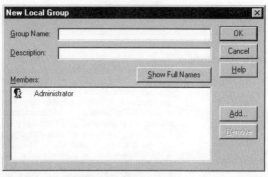

The New Local Group window

New Local Group\\Add

The Add button gives another dialogue box which has two lists: the top list contains the users that the computer system named in the List Names From box knows about. The bottom list contains names of the members that are to be added to the group. To add a new member, a user is selected from the top window and the add button clicked. This can be repeated until the complete list of new members is built up. Clicking the OK button will then add the new members to the group. The members button is dimmed during this operation because the same dialogue box is also used by other utilities to add groups. In this case, the button is not dimmed and if pressed will display the users within a group.

The Add Users and Groups window

<table>
<tr><td></td><td>With the new group created, the main window is updated and the new group added to the bottom list.</td></tr>
<tr><td>**Copy**</td><td>This command will create a duplicate of a user or group and thus make it easier to create a new group. The resulting new group/user will have all the rights of the original it was copied from.</td></tr>
<tr><td>**Delete**</td><td>This command will delete a selected user or group.</td></tr>
<tr><td>**Rename**</td><td>This command will rename a selected user or group.</td></tr>
<tr><td>**Properties**</td><td>This command defines information about the user and is similar to the New User or New Local Group dialogue boxes. It is used to change the properties of the group or user and is allows the Administrator to change the password for a user. If the user forgets the password and cannot log on, the administrator can log on, select the</td></tr>
</table>

user from the main window and then use this command to reset the user's password. Double clicking on the selected user or group within the main window will automatically execute this command and present the Properties dialogue box. The Account Locked Out check box is used to unlock accounts. If someone tries to log on using a user's name and fails to get the correct password, the account can be locked out so that no further attempt to log on using that name will succeed. This policy is set up using the **Policies\\Account** command. If this happens, this check box is marked with a cross. The administrator can remove the lockout by clearing the check box by clicking on it.

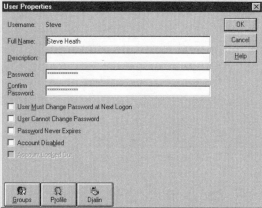

The User Properties window

E<u>x</u>it   This command terminates and closes the User Manager utility.

The Policies menu

The Policies menu determines the security and auditing methods that the system will use. It determines the frequency of password changes, what happens with unsuccessful login attempts and so on. The policies are very important in making the system secure

The Policies menu

<u>A</u>ccount   The account policy is concerned with passwords and log on procedures. The screen shot shows the options that are available. It should be remembered that these apply to the computer as a whole and not to a user or group. The settings shown are for my system for which I am the only real user. These settings are not acceptable for a network where security is important. Most organisations insist on the following settings:

- Password changed regularly (every 60 days).
- Minimum password length of at least 6 characters.
- Old passwords cannot be re-used.
- Account lockout after three log on attempts.
- The Administrator must clear any lockouts.
- Users must log on to be able to change their passwords.

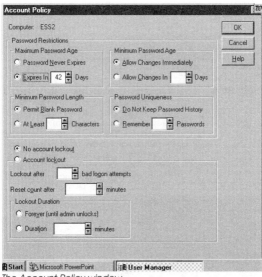

The Account Policy window

User rights

This command allows the users rights to be assigned. Strictly speaking, this command is a little inaccurate in that the rights are typically assigned to groups and then to the users who are members of those groups. The rights are shown in the pull down list and this list can be expanded if the Show Advanced User Rights box is checked. The groups and users that have that right are then displayed in the bottom box. By selecting existing entries within this box and clicking the remove button, the right shown in the Right box is removed from that group or user. To add rights to a user or group, select the right and then click the Add button. This will show the two box dialogue box that has been used to add groups and users in previous User Manager commands (**User\\New Local Group\\Add**). The groups and users are added to the bottom box using this method.

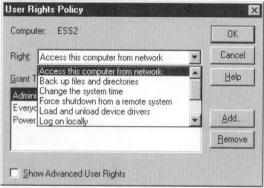

The User Rights Policy window

Audit Policy

The system's audit policy can be defined using this command. The screen shot shows the type of events that can be audited and these are selected by checking the appropriate boxes. The audit events are stored in the event log and can be examined using another administrative tool called the Event Viewer. For the best security, all these events would be audited although this can rapidly create a very large event file!

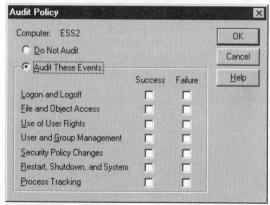

The Audit Policy window

The Options menu

This pulldown menu configures the utility.

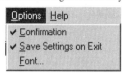

The Options menu

Confirmation
This option determines if confirmation of commands such as **User\\Copy** is required. A tick alongside the menu entry indicates that it is.

Save Settings on Exit
This option if selected will save the settings information when File Manager is exited and thus remember its configuration when it is next opened.

Font
This option displays a font dialogue box that allows the font, size and style used by the utility to be changed.

Disk Administrator

The Disk Administrator is the equivalent to several MS-DOS utilities like FDISK, FORMAT, LABEL and so on. It allows the Administrator to configure and set up disks into various partitions and even extend partitions and volumes by adding disk space from other drives. Many of these techniques depend on the implementation of an NTFS and are not supported if MS-DSO compatible FAT file systems are used instead.

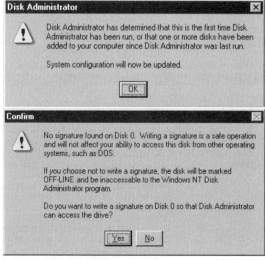

Initial startup messages

When the utility is first used, it displays a coulpe of messages asking for permission to update the system configuration with information about the disks present in the system. It may also update the disks with a signature which provides Disk Administrator with additional information.

The main window lists the physical disk drives that are present in the system and shows how they are partitioned using a bar line and text data. In the screen shot shown, a 1 GB drive is partitioned into two partitions with the primary partition labelled as drive C, using the FAT system and using 400MB. The second partition is configured as free space and using 632 MB disk space. The partitions can be selected by simply clicking in their respective boxes. The selected box border becomes thicker to indicate that it has been selected.

I would recommend backing up data and saving the current disk configuration — use the **Partition\\Configuration\\Save** command — before making any changes using this program. It is very easy to destroy parts of or even all of the file system if the wrong command is used! This command is possible the most dangerous of all the standard commands and utilities because if you get this command wrong, the whole file system is potentially in jeopardy.

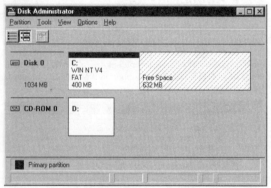

The Disk Administrator main window

The Partition menu

This pull down menu provides a set of commands to handle the creation and deletion of partitions within the system and in this respect is equivalent to the MS-DOS FDISK utility.

Create
This command will do one of two actions: it will create a new primary partition using the free space on the drive starting at the beginning of this area or if an extended partition is selected, it will create a logical drive in that partition. In both cases, a dialogue box will appear asking for the partition size which must be between the minimum and maximum sizes that are also shown in the box.

Create Extended

This command will create a new extended partition using the free space on the drive starting at the beginning of this area. A dialogue box will appear asking for the partition size which must be between the minimum and maximum sizes that are also shown in the box. An extended partition can be configured in a variety of ways and can for example support multiple logical drives. A 200 MB extended partition could be configured as two logical drives of 100 MB each. These drives would be assigned drive letters as normal. This is done after the partition is created by using the **Partition\\Create** command.

Create Volume Set

This command allows an NTFS volume set to be created out disk space on several different drives. This is then treated like a partition which can be assigned to a single or multiple logical drives. Up to 32 disks can be used to create the volume set. Once created it can handled like any other partition. The data is stored sequentially amongst the drives so that the second drive will only be used when the first drive space has been filled up and so on until all the drive spaces have been used. To use this command, the partitions must be selected first. The first partition is selected in the normal way by clicking. The additional partitions on each disk are selected by holding down the CTRL key on the keyboard and selecting them by clicking with the mouse. The system partition cannot be part of the volume set.

Extend Volume Set

This command will extend a selected volume set by allowing more disk space to be added to the volume set and thus increase its size. After this has been completed, the system is reset and the new additional space is formatted. This operation does not affect the original files and thus allows disk partitions to be expanded without having to change path names or any other part of the system, the user or group configurations. To use this command, the partitions must be selected first. The first partition is selected in the normal way by clicking. The additional partitions on each disk are selected by holding down the CTRL key on the keyboard and selecting them by clicking with the mouse. The system partition cannot be part of the volume set and normally uses the FAT file system.

Create Stripe Set

This creates an alternative grouping of multiple disks to create a single volume.

There are more restrictions than compared with the volume set in that the volume is assigned a single drive letter and is not like a partition. The reason is that the volume is created by using a same sized 'stripe' of disk space on each drive in the set and writing the data across the stripes instead of sequentially. To use this command, the partitions must be selected first. The first partition is selected in the normal way by clicking. The additional partitions on each disk are selected by holding down the CTRL key on the keyboard and selecting them by clicking with the mouse. The system partition cannot be part of the stripe set and normally uses the FAT file system.

Mark Active

This command will mark the active partition — the partition with the boot and system files — so that it is used to boot up the system the next time it is restarted. There can only be one active partition at a time. To change the active partition, it is first selected and then this command used. By changing the active partition to another partition, a different operating system can be booted up. However, this can be dangerous if the newly marked partition does not have an operating system or is not the first disk that the system uses to find the boot software.

While 80x86 based Windows NT systems use this concept of the active partition to find the boot software, RISC based machines do not use this concept and the active partition is normally set via a hardware configuration file. The system partition with these machines normally uses the FAT file system.

Configuration

This command is used to save or restore the partitioning information concerning how the disks are set up and configured. This information is important in recovering data from corrupted systems and in providing the ability to go back to a known configuration. It is also a highly dangerous command because it allows different configurations to be restored which if different from the current settings and are committed to, could destroy the data stored on the system! It has three options: save, restore and search. With both the **Restore** and **Search** options, all changes made through the Disk Administrator since opening or the **Commit Changes Now** command was executed will be lost.

Configuration\\Save

This command will save the current configuration information onto a floppy disk. It is a good idea to save the current configuration before making any changes so that the original configuration can be returned to.

Configuration\\Restore

This command will restore the disk configuration information from a floppy disk.

Configuration\\Search

This command will search for other installations of Windows NT — and thus other sets of disk configuration information — and use these to restore the current configuration used by the Disk Administrator

Commit Changes Now

This command will make all the changes that have been made through the Disk Administrator and change the filing system appropriately without having to leave the utility.

Exit

This command closes down the Disk Administrator.

The Tools menu

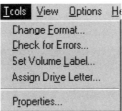

Change Format

This command will format the selected partition and allows the file system to be selected and the drive labelled. The Quick Format option reduces the formatting time by formatting only the disk sectors that require it, but it is sometime less reliable. Before the formatting begins, a warning message will appear saying that this operation will destroy the data that already exists on the drive. This command will not work with the system partition that contains the system files. Any such attempt will result in an error message. This command is not used to format floppy disks: to do this use the **Explorer** and its command **Disk\\Format Disk**.

Format error message

Check for errors This command displays a dialogue box which allows the selected disk to be checked for errors and/or bas sectors.

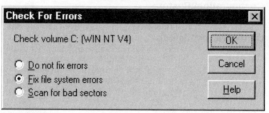

The Check for Errors dialogue box

Set Volume Label This command allows the selected partition or drive to have its label changed.

Assign Drive Letter

This command allows a drive letter to be assigned to a partition so that it can be accessed through the normal file system commands. It can also configure the partition so that a drive letter is not assigned and this is used when other operating systems or applications require special access to the partition without Windows NT from using the partition.

The Assign Drive Letter window

In previous versions, a sperate command was used for CD-ROMs. This is no longer needed because this command will work with CD-ROMs as well as standard hard disks.

The Options menu

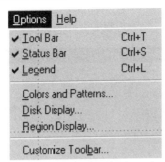

This controls the display options for the main window.

Status Bar
This option if ticked will display the status bar at the bottom of the window.

Legend
This option if ticked will display the legend at the bottom of the window.

Colors and Patterns
This command gives a display box and allows the colours and patterns used to graphically display the size and type or partitions to be configured.

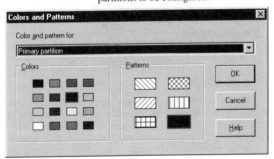

The Colors and Patterns window

Disk Display
This command determines how the disk regions — display boxes — are calculated. They can be determined by the utility itself or based either on actual size or by declaring them to be an equal size.

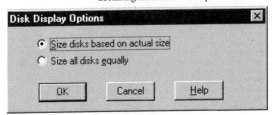

Disk Dispaly dialogue box

<u>R</u>egion Display This command determines how the disk regions — display boxes — are calculated. They can be determined by the utility itself or based either on actual size or by declaring them to be an equal size.

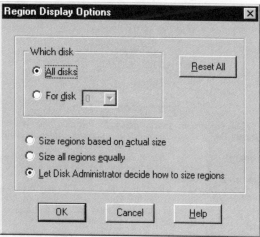

The Region Display window

Customise Tool<u>b</u>ar

This command allows the ToolBar to be customised i.e. icons and their associated commands can be added or removed.

Event Viewer

This utility provides a way of accessing the contents of the various logs that Windows NT provides for storing audit, security and other event information. The data is displayed using a text format and by clicking on an individual entry, a detailed description of that entry can be obtained.

The Event Viewer main window

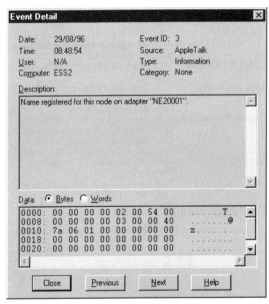

The Event Detail window

The Log menu

This menu controls how the log operates and selects the log type to be viewed.

The Log menu

System	If selected, this window displays the contents of the system log.
Security	If selected, this window displays the contents of the security log.
Application	If selected, this window displays the contents of the application log.

Open	This command will open a previously saved log.
Save As	This saves the current information as a different log file which can be opened using the open command.
Clear All Events	This clears all events form the current display.
Log Settings	This allows the administrator to set up the size of the log file and define the action to be taken when it is full.
Select Computer	This allows the log file of other computers to be examined. The command will display a dialogue box asking for the remote computer to be identified. It is similar to that used to connect a remote drive or printer.
Exit	This command will terminate the utility and close the window.

The View menu

This menu controls how the data is displayed on the screen in the window.

The View menu

All Events	This command will display all specified events.
Filter Events	This command allows the user to specify which events are displayed in the window.
Newest First	If selected, the latest events are at the top of the window.
Oldest First	If selected, the oldest events are at the top of the window.
Find	This command allows the user to search the log for a specific event.
Detail	This is the same as double clicking on an entry. It will display detailed information about the selected event.
Refresh	This updates the display with the latest information from the log files.

The Options menu

This menu controls the options provided by the utility.

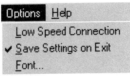

Low Speed Connection

This indicates that the connection to the computer to access the event log is via a low speed modem link. Selecting this option changes the utility's behaviour so that it uses the link bandwidth more efficiently.

Save Settings On Exit

This option if selected will save the utility's settings when the utility is quit.

Font

This allows the display font, size and style to be changed via a dialogue box.

Performance Monitor

This utility provides a lot of information about the system and it performance with respect to many different and selectable parameters such as processing time and the number of page swaps. It can provide and store the information in several ways: as a chart as shown in the screen shot or as a log with entries indicating the status of many internal counters and registers. The logged information can be displayed as a chart at a later date if necessary.

The main use of this utility is in determining where system bottlenecks occur and the effect of changing the system configuration may have. It is possible to determine whether the a poorly performing system is processor performance limited or if the problem is due to large amount of paging out to disk.

The File menu

This menu controls the creation of charts and the saving of settings information.

New Chart

This command will create a new chart and allow a new set of parameters to be monitored.

Open

This command will open a previous settings or log file.

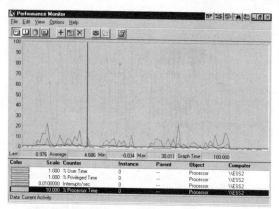

The Performance Monitor main window

<u>S</u>ave Chart Settings

This command saves the current settings as a file. These settings can be opened at a later date and the data defined within the chart can be monitored again.

Save Chart settings <u>A</u>s

This saves the current settings — from another file — to be saved under a different file name as opposed to the original name.

Save <u>W</u>orkspace

This saves the current settings for the utility — not just the settings for the current chart.

<u>E</u>xport Chart

This command will export the chart to other programs for inclusion in presentations and other documents.

E<u>x</u>it

This command terminate the utility and closes the window.

The Edit menu

This pull down menu controls the content of the chart.

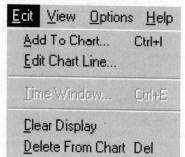

The Edit menu

Add to Chart

This command will add data lines to the chart. A display box comes up which allows the data to be monitored to be chosen and the characteristics of its data line on the chart to be set up.

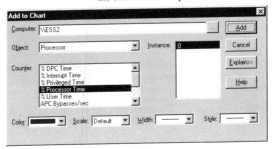

The Add to Chart window

This includes the size, width and colour of the line. The data is selected from a combination of the object and counter pulldown lists. The object part of the system while the Counter entry defines a performance parameter about the object. The Explain button if clicked, will display a text box describing the counter and object that has been chosen.

Edit Chart Line

This command will allow the current selected chart line to be edited. It is similar to the previous box, except that the only characteristics that can be changed, are its appearance.

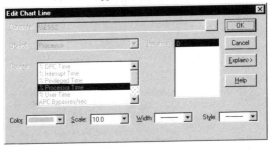

The Edit Chart Line window

Time Window
This command defines the time window that will be used to collect data.

Clear Display
This command clears the current chart.

Delete from Chart
This command will delete the current selected chart line from the chart.

The View menu

This command allows the logged data to be displayed in several different ways.

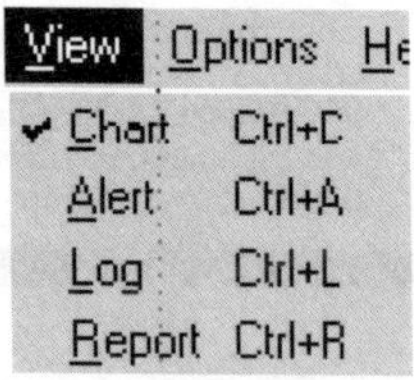

The View menu

Chart	If selected, the window will display the current chart
Alert	If selected, the window shows a list of recent alert messages.
Log	If selected, the window shows the log that contains the information that is used as the base for the chart. This information is displayed using a text format.
Report	This command displays a report based on the parameters captured for the log/chart.

The Options menu

This pull down menu selects the different options that the utility supports.

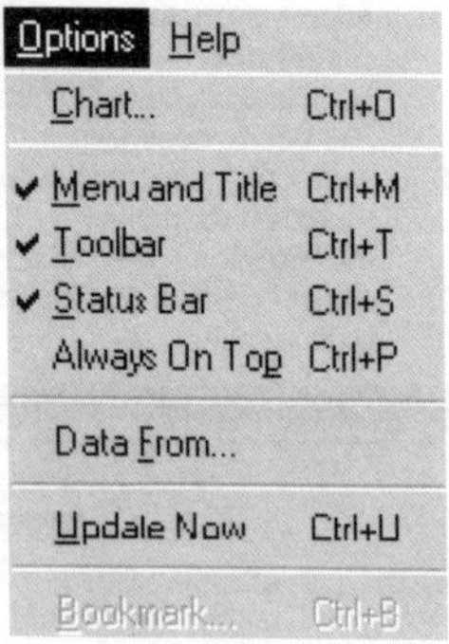

The Options menu

Chart	This command displays a dialogue box where the chart options can be set up. They include the inclusion of a legend, vertical and horizontal grid lines and the update method.
Menu and title	If selected, this displays both the menu bar and title within the window.
Toolbar	If selected this displays the toolbar.
Statusbar	If selected this displays the status bar.
Always on Top	If selected this ensures that the Performance Monitor window is always visible and is not hidden by other windows, even when it is not in the foreground.
Data From	This command will allow data to be viewed from either the current log file or from a previously saved log file.

Update Now This command forces the data within the display to be updated.

Bookmark This creates a bookmark within the log for future referencing.

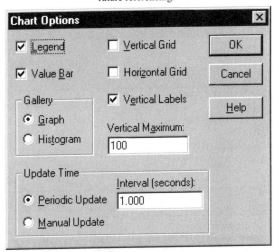

The Chart Option window

Backup

This utility uses tape devices to backup the contents of the disks on the system to tape and unlike its MS-DOS predecessor, cannot backup to floppy disks. The utility removes the need to have a specialised tape based backup utility which is the case with Windows 3.11 and MS-DOS. The disadvantage is that it predominantly works with a SCSI based tape drive and is therefore not compatible with many of the PC based tape drives that use the floppy disk port, parallel port or even their own interface card.

The utility requires that a tape device is connected and this can be done either as part of the installation process or by using the Windows NT Setup utility in the Main Program Group. Please note that to back up *all* the system, you must be logged on as a member of the Backup group and not simply as the administrator.

Installing a tape drive

This is performed using the **Tape devices** control panel. It performs the installation and configuration of tape streamers primarily attached to the SCSI bus, but also including some of the IDE and Floppy based controllers as well.

The Devices sub-panel displays a list of installed devices and through the **Properties** button can allow a selected device to be configured.

The Drivers sub-panel allows drivers to be installed and/or deleted. If new hardware or a tape streamer has been added, then this panel must be used to install the appropriate driver and configure it. The installation normally requires a system restart to make the driver software and thus the tape streamer available to the system. The Backup utility, provided in the Administrator's toolkit, can access the tape streamers and backup/restore the data stored on the system, either on local disks or across the network.

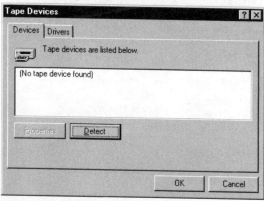

The Drivers sub-panel

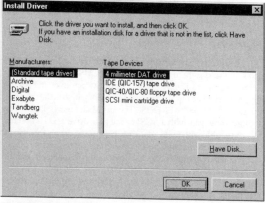

The Tape streamer list

The Backup main window

Opening the utility will present the main window as shown here. It is similar in style to the File Manager and has several smaller windows: the Drives window displays icons of all the drives, the Tapes window displays icons of any tapes that the system knows about and by double clicking on the drive icons, a third window appears that displays the drives contents using a similar method to that used by the Explorer.

If nor tape drive is installed, then the utility will still open but an error message will appear as shown explaining how to install a tape drive.

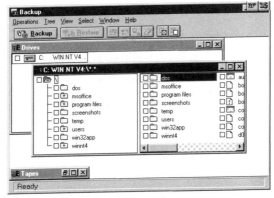

The main window (2 windows open)

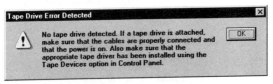

A Backup error message

Selecting files

Many of the commands within Backup require files to be
selected. The same techniques used within the File Manager will
work here e.g. To select a single file, simply place the cursor over
the file or directory name and click once. The name will be
highlighted. Dragging the cursor over multiple names with the
mouse button down will select multiple files. The same effect can
also be achieved by selecting individual files while holding down
the SHIFT key. However, Backup also provides check boxes
which can also be clicked and effectively mark the file or directory
for backup. Selected or highlighted files can also be marked for
backup by using the **Select\\Check** command.

The Operations menu

This menu provides the basic backup commands and operations for the tape.

Backup	This command will backup the selected disks to tape.
Restore	This command will restore the contents of the selected tape to a specified disk or directory within the file system.
Catalog	This will display a catalogue of the tape's contents. Depending on the tape technology used, this can take some time.
Erase Tape	This will erase the selected tape. This destroys its contents and should be used with care.

Re_tension Tape
This command will retension the tape and it is advisable when using a new tape to retension it several times to remove any tape stretch which could cause a lose of data.

E_ject Tape
This will eject the tape from the tape mechanism. Not all tape drives support this command and some tapes have to have their tape cartridge ejected manually.

_Format Tape
This command will format the tape and is optional depending on the tape technology.

_Hardware Setup
This configures the hardware setup for the tape drive.

E_xit
This command closes the utility.

The Tree menu

This menu controls the display of the filing system.

E_xpand One Level
This command will expand the current level — drive C — by one level so that all the directories immediately below it are visible.

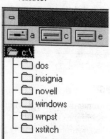

Expand _Branch
This command will expand the current directory or branch — the directory 'windows' — by one level so that all the directories immediately below it are visible.

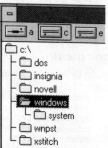

Expand _All
This command will expand the current level — drive C — by one level so that all the directories and sub-directories below it are visible.

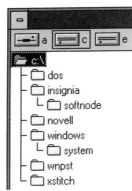

Collapse Branch   This is the reverse of the **Expand All** command and hides all the directories and sub-directories below the selected part of the tree.

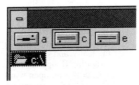

The View menu

Tree and Directory If this is clicked, it shows both the tree and directory structures.

Tree Only   If this is clicked, it displays only the tree structure.

Directory Only   If this is clicked, it displays only the directory.

Split   This splits the window.

All File Details This option gives all file details.

Status Bar   If this is clicked, the status bar is displayed.

Toolbar   If this is clicked, the Toolbar is displayed.

Font   This allows the display font, its size and style to be changed.

The Select menu

This menu controls the selection or de-selection of disks, files and directories for backup.

C̲heck This command will mark any selected files, directories or disks for backup by checking their respective check boxes which appear alongside their names.

U̲ncheck This command will unmark any selected files, directories or disks and thus remove them from the list for backup, This is indicated by clearing their respective check boxes which appear alongside their names.

The Window Menu

This command controls the windows and the its appearance.

C̲ascade Arranges open windows so that the title bar of each window is visible.

T̲ile Arranges all the open windows side by side so that all of them are visible.

A̲rrange Icons Arranges all selected items or icons into rows.

R̲efresh This will update the file structure shown in the window. This does not happen automatically and can cause problems when swapping floppy or removable disks.

C̲lose All This closes all open windows.

1̲,2̲,3̲ etc. The remaining commands allow the user to select any one of the open windows. This can also be done by directly clicking on the appropriate window.

Windows NT Diagnostics

The Windows NT Diagnostics is a utility that provide detailed information concerning the current system and its configuration. Much of the information is beyond the scope of the pocket book and concerns the internal workings of the operating system. However, this utility does have a lot of basic configuration information which is often needed or used by technical support lines. To show where this information can be obtained, the main diagnostic windows have been included with a simple explanation of the information that they contain. For more details, refer back to the documentation supplied with the Windows NT software.

Version

This gives information about the operating system installation and includes the installation date, revision number, the registered owner and so on.

The build number indicates the actual revision number and not the revision number. Microsoft issues pre-releases of it operating system to beta testers and developers which will have the same revision number but an earlier build number. This information can be important to for technical support as a bug may appear in one build and not in another.

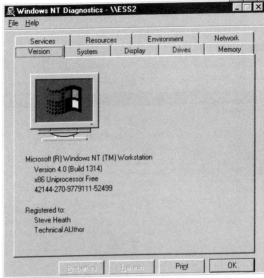

The Version sub-panel

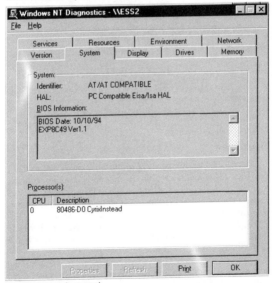

The System sub-panel

System

This window gives information about the BIOS and Video ROMs and describes the processor type and configuration. The system that the screen shot was taken from, is based on a generic

PCI/ISA motherboard using Cyrix 586 processor. More specific systems and processors from recognised manufacturers may have a different IDs and descriptions.

Memory

This window should give details about the memory used in the system, including information on the virtual memory file.

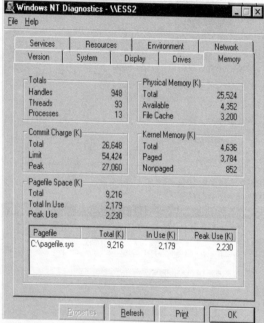

The Memory sub-panel

Services

The Services sub-panel is similar to a driver list in that it provides a list of services that the system is currently running. Such services include the Event Log and Print spooler services. Again their status is shown and by double clicking on an entry in the window, more detailed information can be displayed.

It can display information either on services or hardware devices. The choice is made by clicking on the appropriate button at the bottom of the window.

If a service cannot be accessed, it is useful to check through this window that the appropriate driver has been installed. Typically the driver name will have some resemblance to the device e.g. floppy, AppleTalk and so on. In some cases, the driver name is based on the chip that is used on the plug-in card. This is the case with the Future Domain SCSI card whose driver is named after the SCSI chip i.e. FD8xx.

If a driver is double clicked, or selected and the **Properties** button clicked, more detailed information is shown in a window to that below. This gives further information about its dependencies and error control.

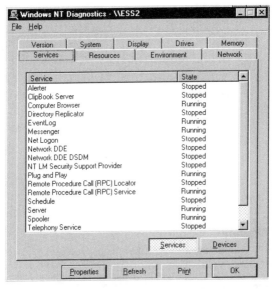

The Services sub-panel

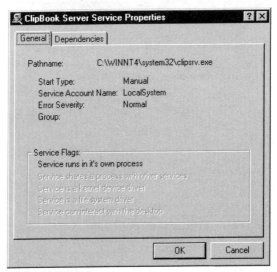

The Services Properties

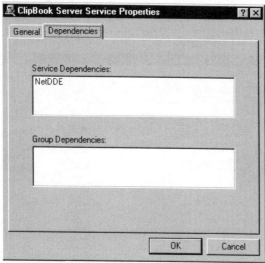

The Services Properties (ii)

Display

This provide information about the graphics card(s) installed in the system and includes the BIOS information, and the current settings. The settings are changed using the **Display** control panel.

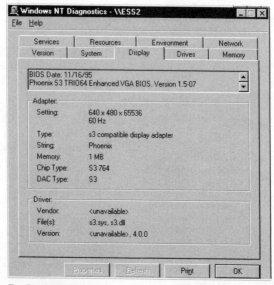

The Display sub-panel

Drives

This provide information about the disk drives present in the system. All of the drives present in the system including floppy drives, CD-ROMs and hard disk drives appear in the list, identified by their assigned disk drive letter. Selecting a drive entry and clicking the Properties button gives more information about the drive such as its size, file system type and free and used space.

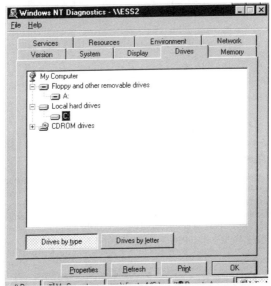

The Drives sub-panel

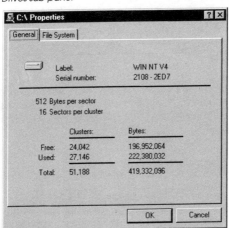

The Drives General Properties window

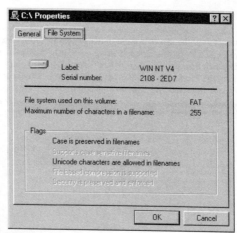

The Drive File System Properties window

Resources

This is used to identify the low level hardware and the resources i.e. I/O addresses, interrupt levels and so on that have been assigned to a resource. It is useful in both identifying conflicts and free interrupt levels and I/O addresses. Different resource types can be displayed by clicking the appropriate button and a resource's properties can be shown by double-clicking on an entry in the window or selecting it and using the **Properties** button.

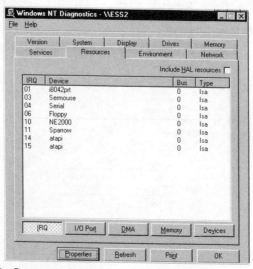

The Resources sub-panel

Environment

This window provides information about the system environment such as the number of processors, operating system software revision numbers, paths and so on.

By clicking the Local User button, similar information can be shown for the local user(s) as well. This information can be obtained and/or changed by using the **System** control panel as well.

This type of information is often requested by technical support helplines to allow them to identify that all the paths through the file system have been correctly set up for an application to use. This can also require environment variables to be set up as well.

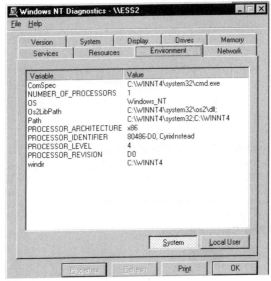

The Environment sub-panel

Network

This sub-panel gives a lot of information about the system network characteristics including a set of statistics about the amount of data that has been sent and the success/failure rate. As the screen shot overleaf shows, this particular system has noty been very active due to the fact that the screen shot was taken just after it was set up.

The buttons at the bottom of the sub-panel allow the different types of information to be displayed. The **Settings** button will show the current network settinmgs although this cannot be changed from this utility. The **Network** control panel must be used instead.

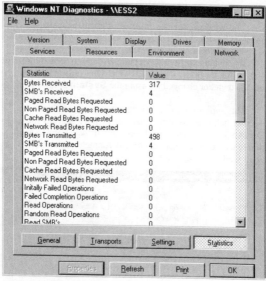

The Network sub-panel

Remote Access Admin

This utility is used to control any remote access via a telephone line instead of using a direct network connection such as an Ethernet or Token Ring link. The window shows any active and connected remote users and allows the remote access permissions and server configuration to be changed.

The Server menu

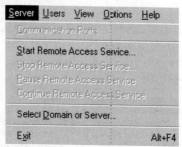

Communication Ports

This commands defines and sets up which ports are to be used.

Start Remote Access Service

This command will start up the remote access and allow someone to remotely connect.

S**t**opRemote Access Service

> This command will stop the remote access and prevent someone from remotely accessing the system.

Pause Remote Access Service

> This command will pause up the remote access.

Co**n**tinue Remote Access Service

> This command will continue the remote access.

Select **D**omain or Server

> This command will allow a particular domain or server to be selected if the network provides more than one.

E**x**it

> This exits the utility.

The Users menu

Permissions

> This command will show the permissions for users.

Active Users

> This command will show active i.e. connected users.

The Options menu

Low Speed Connection

> This indicates that the connection to the computer to access the event log is via a low speed modem link. Selecting this option changes the utility's behaviour so that it uses the link bandwidth more efficiently.

Save Settings On Exit

> This option if selected will save the utility's settings when the utility is quit.

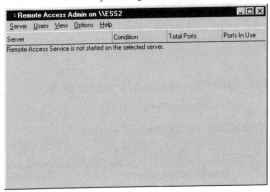

The Main window

10   How do I do that?

This chapter is a list of the common activities and operations that users want to perform within Windows NT and gives simple sets of bullets on how to do them. If you want to find out more, then refer back to the utilities described in the other chapters for additional detail. In some cases, there are several methods. Each bulleted item is a separate method.

Changing the system

Changing the desktop

- To change the colours used in the desktop, open the **Display** control panel and select the **Color** sub-panel.

- To change the background and so on, open the **Display** control panel and use the **Desktop** sub-panel.

Changing the video

- To change the size and colour resolution of the video e.g. to move from 640 by 480 to 800 by 600, open the **Display** control panel and use the **Settings** sub-panel.

Changing the environmental variables

- Open the **System** control panel. The environmental variables are displayed in the bottom two boxes and can then be modified.

Changing the boot up procedure

- Open the **System** control panel and use the **Desktop** sub-panel. The names and time out period used during system boot are shown at the top of the window and can be modified.

Changing the date and time formats

- Open the **Date/Time** control panel.

Changing the keyboard layout

- Open the **Windows NT Setup** utility in the Main program group and use the **Options\\Change Mouse or Keyboard** command.

Changing the mouse settings

- To install a different mouse, open **the Windows NT Setup** utility in the Main program group and use the **Options\\Change Mouse or Keyboard** command.

- To change the current mouse settings e.g. speed, resoulution and so on, open the **Mouse** control panel.

Changing the sound settings

- Open the **Sounds** control panel to assign different sounds to system beeps and so on.

Changing the disk configurations

- Open the **Disk Administrator** utility in the Administrator Tools program.

Adding/removing tape drives

- If a new controller has been added to support the drive, the controller must be installed first. Open the **Tape Devices** control panel and select the **Drivers** sub-panel and use the **Add or Remove** buttons.

Adding/removing SCSI drives and CD-ROMs

- If a new drive controller has been added to support the drive, the controller must be installed first. Open the **SCSI Devices** control panel and select the **Drivers** sub-panel and use the **Add or Remove** buttons. After this installation, open the **Disk Administrator** utility in the Administrator Tools program group, partition the disk — **Partition\\Create** — and then format it using **Tools\\Format**.

- If a new CD-ROM controller has been added to support the drive, the controller must be installed first. Open the **SCSI Devices** control panel and select the **Drivers** sub-panel and use the **Add or Remove** buttons.

Files and directories
Copying

- Open the **Explorer, My Computer** or other window, select the files and drag them to their destination drive or directory icon using the *right hand* button. This will display a menu where the copy command can be selected.

- Open the **MS-DOS** prompt and use the **Copy** command.

Deleting

- Open the **Explorer, My Computer** or other window, select the files and press the DEL key.

- Open the **Explorer, My Computer** or other window, select the files use the **File\\Delete** command.

- Open the **MS-DOS** prompt and use the **Delete** command.

Renaming

- Open the **Explorer, My Computer** or other window, select the files use the **File\\Rename** command.

- Open the **MS-DOS** prompt and use the **Rename** command.

Moving

- Open the **Explorer, My Computer** or other window, select the files and drag them to their destination drive or directory icon using the *right hand* button. This will display a menu where the copy command can be selected.

Backing up

- For small files, open the **Explorer, My Computer** or other window and copy the files to another disk drive or floppy disk by selecting them and dragging them to their new destination drive or folder.

- For large files and complete disks, use the **Backup** utility in the Administrative Tools program group.

- To make a copy of a disk, open the **My Computer**, select the disk to be copied from the window and then use the **File\\Copy Disk** command.

Finding

- Open the **Explorer, My Computer** or other window, use the **File\\Find** command.

- Open the **Explorer** use the **Tools\\Find** command.

- Use the **MS-DOS** prompt and the **Dir** command.

Adding more disk space

- To add more space to an existing disk drive, open the **Disk Administrator** utility in the Administrator Tools program group select the drive that needs to be expanded and use the **Partition\\Extend Volume Set** command. If this is dimmed out, extending the size of the drive is not possible.

- If an additional drive has been added to the existing disk controller, open the **Disk Administrator** utility in the Administrator Tools program group, partition the disk — **Partition\\Create** — and then format it using **Tools\\Format**.

- If a new controller has been added to support the drive, the controller must be installed first. Open the **Windows NT Setup** utility in the Main program group and

use the **Options\\Add\Remove SCSI controllers**
command. After this installation, open the **Disk Administrator** utility in the Administrator Tools program
group, partition the disk — **Partition\\Create** — and
then format it using **Tools\\Format**.

Keyboard alternatives

Moving to different buttons

• Pressing the TAB key will move the highlight to the next
item e.g. the next button in a dialogue box, the next folder
in an open window and so on.

• Pressing the cursor keys ($\uparrow \downarrow \leftarrow \rightarrow$) will move the
highlight to the next item e.g. the next choice where
'radio' style buttons are used such as the shutdown box.

Using the keyboard instead of a mouse

• Pressing the ALT key will activate the menu bar. Press
the underlined letter in the required menu name and the
pull down menu will drop down. The command can be
selected by using the cursor keys to move the highlight
or by pressing the underlined letter in the required
command name. Pressing TAB with a menu pulled
down, will close the current menu and open the next one.

• Pressing the ENTER key has the same action as clicking
on the currently selected button or icon.

Navigating the screen

Selecting other applications

• Hold down the ALT key and press the TAB key. A small
window will appear with the icon of the next task or
application in the task list. If the ALT key is released, that
task is brought to the foreground. If the TAB key is
released and pressed again, the next task is displayed and
so on.

• If the window or just a part of a window of the required
task or application is visible, just click on it.

• Press the CNTRL and ESC keys together to display the
Start button menu. Select the required menu item by
using the $\uparrow$ and $\downarrow$ keys. To move into the next menu use
the $\leftarrow$ and $\rightarrow$ keys.

• Pressing the CNTRL, ALT and DEL keys
simultanaeously will present a dialogue box where one
of the options is to present the task list. With the task list,
the task or application can be selected as previously
described.

Deleting other tasks

- Close the task window. This will exit the task and delete it from the current task list.

- Use the Exit command which is typically the last command in the first pull down menu.

- Pressing the CNTRL, ALT and DEL keys simultaneously will present a dialogue box where one of the options is to present the task list. With the task list, the task or application can be selected as previously described.

Minimise and maximise windows

- The first method uses the up and down buttons on the top right of the window.

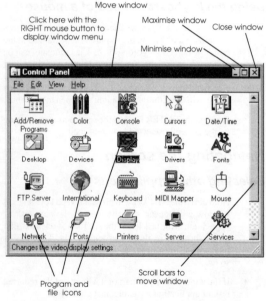

Move window

Click here with the
RIGHT mouse button to
display window menu

Maximise window

Close window

Minimise window

Program and
file icons

Scroll bars to
move window

- Double clicking on the top bar of the window will maximise it..

- The second method uses the Minimise and Maximise commands from the window pull down menu as shown.

Adjusting windows

- Place the cursor over the edge of the window, hold the

mouse button down, wait for it to change to the double headed arrow cursor and move the mouse. The window will chnage size as required.

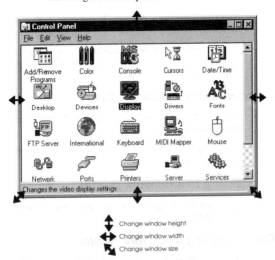

> Change window height
> Change window width
> Change window size

- The second method uses the Size command from the window pull down menu.

Creating a program group or item

- Go to the **Start** button and use the **Settings\\Taskbar** command. Select the **Start Menu Programs** sub panel from the resulting dialogue box. Then use the **Add** command to add the group or item.

Deleting a program group

- Go to the **Start** button and use the **Settings\\Taskbar** command. Select the **Start Menu Programs** sub panel from the resulting dialogue box. Then use the **Remove** command and select the group to be removed.

Deleting a program item

- Go to the **Start** button and use the **Settings\\Taskbar** command. Select the **Start Menu Programs** sub panel from the resulting dialogue box. Then use the **Remove** command and then select the item to be removed.

Networks

Connecting to a network drive

- Open the **Explorer** and use the **Tools\\Map Network Drive** command.

- Open the **Network Neighborhood** and select the network files or drive that is needed by selecting the appropriate icon(s) and opening them.

Disconnecting a network drive

- Open the **Explorer** and use the **Tools\\Disconnect Network Drive** command.

- Close the windows opened through the **Network Neighborhood**.

Connecting to a network printer

- Open the **Printers** control panel and open the **Add Printer** file.

Disconnecting a network printer

- Open the **Printers** control panel, select the icon of the network printer to be disconnected and use the **File\\Delete** command.

Adding/removing network boards and drivers

- Use the **Network** control panel.

Passwords

Changing

- Open the **User Manager** utility in the Administrative Tools program group, and double click on the user that needs the password to be changed. The **User Properties** box will appear and the password can be changed.

Forgotten

- Open the **User Manager** utility in the Administrative Tools program group, and double click on the user that needs the password to be changed. The **User Properties** box will appear and the password can be changed. Inform the user of the new password.

Locked out accounts

- Open the **User Manager** utility in the Administrative

Tools program group, and double click on the user that needs the password to be changed. The **User Properties** box will appear and the account unlocked by unchecking the **Account Locked Out** box.

Screen savers

- Open the **Display** control panel. and select the **Screensavers** sub-panel. This allows the screen saver to be enabled and if needed password protected.

Printing

Creating a printer

- Open the **Printers** control panel and open the **Add Printer** file.

Accessing a printer on another system

- Open the **Printers** control panel and open the **Add Printer** file.

Assigning the default printer

- Open the **Printers** control panel and open the icon of the required printer. To set the printer as the default, use the **Printers\\Set as Default Printer** command.

Using a different printer

- Open the **Printers** control panel and open the icon of the required printer. To set the printer as the default, use the **Printers\\Set as Default Printer** command.

- Most applications have the ability in the **Print** or **Print Setup** commands to select a different printer.

Deleting documents

- Open the **Printers** control panel and open the icon of the required printer. Select a document and then use the **Document\\Cancel** command. Alternatively press the DEL key once the document has been selected.

Pausing a printer

- Open the **Printers** control panel and open the icon of the required printer. From within the resulting window, use the **Printer\\Pause** command.

- Open the **Printers** control panel and selectthe icon of the required printer. From within the resulting window, use the **File\\Pause Printing** command.

Resuming a paused printer

- Open the **Printers** control panel and open the icon of the required printer. From within the resulting window, use the **Printer\\Resume** command.

- Open the **Printers** control panel and select the icon of the required printer. From within the resulting window, use the **File\\Pause Printing** command.

Pausing a document

- Open the **Printers** control panel and open the icon of the required printer. From within the resulting window, use the **Printer\\Pause** command.

Resuming a document

- Open the **Printers** control panel and open the icon of the required printer. From within the resulting window, select a document and then use the **Document\\Resume** command.

Setting up the printer

- Open the **Printers** control panel and open the icon of the required printer. and use the **Printer\\Properties** command.

Page sizes

- Open the **Printers** control panel and open the icon of the required printer and use the **Printer\\Properties** command.

Screen dumps

- To copy the whole screen to the Clipboard, where it can be pasted into a document, press the **Print Screen** key.

- To copy the current window — not the whole screen — to the Clipboard, where it can be pasted into a document, press the **Alt** and **Print Screen** keys together.

- When pasting screen dumps into a Word or Powerpoint document, the image will be automatically scaled to fit the paper size.

A Hayes compatible modem commands

Standard AT commands

Please note that the prefix AT must not be forgotten. Without it, the modem does not interpret the data as a command and will ignore it. Commands will also be treated like data if the modem is on-line. To force it off line and thus able to accept and process commands, enter +++.

ATA The A command forces the modem to go off-hook in answer mode and effectively answers an incoming call.

ATBn This command determines which communication standard is preferred for the next connection.

    0   CCITT mode

    1   Bell 103 and Bell 212A, instead of V.21 and V.22, in case of fallback (default)

ATD This is the most commonly used AT command and will dial a telephone number.

    T   Select tone dialling. (default).

    P   Selects pulse dialling, with the dialling speed fixed at 10 pulses per second.

    ,   The comma modifier introduces a delay time before dialling the next dial character or executing the next character in the dial string. The pause time is the value of the S8 register, (default=2 seconds).

    W   The W modifier makes the modem wait for a dial tone before sending the next digit. Useful when dialling through a PABX or when there is a delay in getting an outside line.

    :   The colon is used to request that a calling card is detected. Place the colon in the dial string and the card number after it.

    @   For the time specified in the S7 register (default=50 seconds), the modem attempts to detect 5 seconds of silence.

    !   The exclamation mark causes the modem to go on-hook then back off-hook, as if the receiver on the telephone set had been pressed momentarily.

    R   The R modifier changes the modem from originate mode to answer mode after the dialling process is complete. This command is used only at the end of the dial string.

      ;   Return to local command state after dialling. This can be used to get the modem to dial number without the modem taking over the line. Once connected, the call can be handled by a hand set for example.

ATS=n Dial telephone number stored at location n Dials telephone number stored in location n, where n is 0, 1,or 2. You must have previously saved the value with the AT&Z command.

ATEn This turns on or off the echoing of data back to the PC. This can be the cause of the modem failing to respond if echo is turned off. If multiple echoes are received, use this command to switch it off.

      0   Turns off the echo command.

      1   Turns on the echo command. This allows you to see that characters you have sent to the modem have been received and sent back. (default)

ATHn This command hangs up the modem and disconnects it. To issue the command, first enter the +++ sequence to before sending the hang up command, ATH.

      0   Forces the modem on-hook. Disconnects the modem from the telephone line and ends any current call.

      1   Forces the modem off-hook.

ATIn Gets information about the modem depending on the value of n.

      0   Asks the modem for its product ID code.

      1   Returns a modem code.

      2   Returns OK.

      3   Returns the modem's country code.

      4   Returns a list of modem features.

      9   Returns product code and firmware version of the modem. This is not always supported.

ATLn Speaker volume

      0   Low speaker volume.

      1   Low speaker volume.

      2   Medium speaker volume.

      3   High speaker volume.

ATMn Speaker on/off/auto

      0   Disables speaker.

      1   Turns on the speaker until carrier is established. (default)

	2	Leaves the speaker on throughout the entire connection.
	3	Turns the speaker on until a carrier is detected, except during dialling.

ATNn Communication protocol preference Sets the modem protocol.

	0	Use S37 for speed selection. If S37=0, connect at highest possible speed. Otherwise, connect at speed specified in S37.
	1	Connect at speed set in S37. Fallback if necessary. (default)
	2	Same as N1 for compatibility reasons.

ATOn Returns modem to on-line state from command state.

	0	Is used to return to the on-line state after having entered the command state using the escape sequence.
	1	Same as above and will retrain the carrier (possibly at a lower speed) before reentering on-line state.

ATP Enable pulse dialling. This sets the default dialling mode to pulse mode. This command can also be used as a subcommand of the D command.

ATQn Quiet (refer to command Vn)

	0	Allows result codes to be sent to your screen. (default)
	1	Turns off the result code messages.
	2	Returns result codes when originating a call, but not when answering.

ATSn Select an S register. The S registers refer to memory locations used for configuration. The S commands are used to assign values to various registers in the modem's memory.

	n?	The Sn? command (n=register number) is used for checking the contents of a register. The result is always expressed as a three-digit number, where the leading digits or all digits may be 0.
	Sn=r	This is used to change an S register value (where n is the number of the register and r is the assigned value).

ATT Sets the default dialling mode to tone dialling instead of pulse. Often used within a dialling string e.g. ATDT 0123 345 678

ATVn This command defines how returned messages are formatted. For most uses, the verbal method i.e. test based messages is the most frequently used and expected.

0	Displays result messages as code numbers (nonverbal).
1	Displays result messages as English words (verbal, default)

The code numbers and their meanings are:

0	OK Command is correct and has been completed
1	CONNECT Connection established
2	RING Incoming ring detected
3	NO CARRIER No connection or lost the carrier
4	ERROR Bad command
5	CONNECT 1200 Connection established at 1200 bps
6	NO DIALTONE Dial tone not detected in S7 seconds
7	BUSY Busy tone detected
8	NO ANSWER See ATD . . .@. . .
10	CONNECT 2400 Connection established at 2400 bps
11	CONNECT 4800 Connection established at 4800 bps
12	CONNECT 9600 Connection established at 9600 bps
13	CONNECT 14400 Connection established at 14400 bps
15	CONNECT 7200 Connection established at 7200 bps
16	CONNECT 12000 Connection established at 12000 bps
24	CONNECT 300/REL Connection with MNP 300 bps
25	CONNECT 1200/REL Connection with MNP 1200 bps
26	CONNECT 2400/REL Connection with MNP 2400 bps
27	CONNECT 4800/REL Connection with MNP 4800 bps
28	CONNECT 9600/REL Connection with MNP 9600 bps
29	CONNECT 7200/REL Connection with MNP 7200 bps

30	CONNECT 12000/REL Connection with MNP 12000 bps
31	CONNECT 14400/REL Connection with MNP 14400 bps
40	CARRIER 300 Carrier detected at 300 bps
46	CARRIER 1200 Carrier detected at 1200 bps
47	CARRIER 2400 Carrier detected at 2400 bps
48	CARRIER 4800 Carrier detected at 4800 bps
49	CARRIER 7200 Carrier detected at 7200 bps
50	CARRIER 9600 Carrier detected at 9600 bps
51	CARRIER 12000 Carrier detected at 12000 bps
52	CARRIER 14400 Carrier detected at 14400 bps
66	COMPRESSION: CLASS 5 MNP class 5
67	COMPRESSION: V.42BIS V.42 bis compression
69	COMPRESSION:NONE No compression
70	PROTOCOL:NONE Asynchronous mode
77	PROTOCOL:LAP-M Error control mode with LAP-M protocol
80	PROTOCOL:ALT Error control mode with MNP protocol
128	MODEM IN USE Modem already in use for this or another application

ATWn The ATW setting determines whether progress result codes are displayed in addition to the ATX codes. Register S95 determines which progress result codes will be displayed.

0	Progress codes 40 through 80 disabled.
1	Progress codes 40 through 80 enabled. (default)
2	Progress codes enabled; identical to W1.

ATXn Active result code

0	Selects result codes 0 through 4 and 8.
1	Selects result codes 0 through 5, 8, and 10 through 28.
2	Selects result codes 0 through 6, 8, and 10 through 28.
3	Selects result codes 0 through 5, 7, 8, and 10 through 28.
4	Selects all result codes. (default)

ATYn This command sets modem behaviour for responding to a long break signal.

> 0   The modem ignores any long breaks received from the remote modem. (default)
>
> 1   On receiving a long break from the remote modem, the modem goes on-hook (hangs up), and returns to command state.
>
> 2   On receiving a long break from the remote modem, the modem returns to command state, but remains connected to the remote modem (does not hang up).

ATZn This command resets the modem. Many terminal programs do this automatically before dialling.

> 0   Loads Profile 0 into the active profile.
>
> 1   Loads Profile 1 into the active profile.

AT&Cn

> DCD options. Some modems do not support this command and return OK for compatibility.
>
> 0   DCD is always on.
>
> 1   DCD is on when the data carrier is detected but off when the carrier is not detected.

AT&Dn

> DTR options. Some modems do not support this command and return OK for compatibility.
>
> 0   Modem ignores DTR.
>
> 1   Modem will go into the command state if an on-off transition is detected on DTR.
>
> 2   Modem will hang up, go into the command state, and disable auto-answering if an on-off transition is detected on DTR.
>
> 3   Modem initialises if an on-off transition is detected on DTR.

AT&F Recall default profile The current active profile is replaced by the default factory configuration.

AT&Gn

> Guard tones are used in some telephone systems to allow proper data transfer over the network. Guard tones are not used in the United States.
>
> 0   Disables guard tone. (default)
>
> 1   Same as 2.
>
> 2   Sends 1800 Hz guard tone.

AT&Kn

This command specifies which kind of local flow control is used. Many modems do not support this command and return OK for compatibility.

0-5   Respond OK, no action taken

AT&Ln

This command affects the modem's behaviour during the call setup and the carrier handshake phases at the beginning of a connection.

0   Selects switched (dial-up) line. (default)

1   Selects conditioned leased line.

AT&Pn

Pulse mode make/break ratio

0   Sets the dial pulse make/break ratio at 39%/ 61% (10 pps, USA/Canada).

1   Sets the dial pulse make/break ratio at 33%/ 67% (10 pps, UK/HongKong).

2   Sets the dial pulse make/break ratio at 39%/ 61% (20 pps).

3   Sets the dial pulse make/break ratio at 33%/ 67% (20 pps).

AT&Qn

This command allows you to enable and disable error control mode. This command has precedence over setting registers S36 and S48.

0   Asynchronous mode (no error control, disables V.42 and MNP).

5   Error control mode Instructs the modem to make a connection using V.42/MNP, and fallback as necessary.

AT&Rn

CTS/RTS Many modems do not support this command and return OK for compatibility.

0–1   Return OK.

AT&Sn

DSR Many modems do not support this command and return OK for compatibility.

0–2   Return OK.

AT&Tn

These diagnostic self tests are available only when no error protocol is engaged. The duration of each test is controlled by register S18.

0	Terminate the test
1	Local analog loopback
3	Local digital loopback
4	Enable the remote digital loopback
5	Disable the remote digital loopback
6	Remote digital loopback test
7	Remote digital loopback with self-test
8	Local analog loopback with self-test

AT&Un

This command turns on or off Trellis code modulation in V.32.

0	Enable Trellis coding. (default)
1	Disable Trellis coding.

A   T   &   V   n

Displays the modem profile and stored telephone numbers:

> Active profile
> Stored profile 0
> Stored profile 1
> Stored telephone numbers (See AT&Z.)

AT&Wn

This command saves the current modem profile into either profile 0 or 1.

0	Saves the active profile into profile 0.
1	Saves the active profile into profile 1.

AT&Yn

Specify start-up profile Allows choosing between two different configurations at start-up.

0	Specifies saved profile 0 as start-up configuration.
1	Specifies saved profile 1 as start-up configuration.

AT&Zn=s

Stores the phone number into one of the three storage registers 0,1 or 2..

S register descriptions

No:	Description	Default	Range
S0	Number of rings to auto answer	0	0:255
S1	Ring counter	0	0:255
S2	Escape Character	43 <+>	0:127
S3	Line-termination character	13 <CR>	0:127
S4	Line-feed character	10 <LF>	0:127
S5	Backspace character	8 <BS>	0:127
S6	Blind dialling wait (seconds)	2	2:255
S7	Carrier wait	50	1:255
S8	Pause time	2	0:255
S9	Carrier detect response time(0.1s)	6	1:255
S10	Disconnect timing (0.1s)	14	1:255
S11	Duration for DTMFdialing(ms)	95	50:255
S12	Escape code guard time (0.02 s)	50	20:255
S18	Self-test duration (seconds)	0	0:255
S36	Negotiation failure treatment	5	

Specifies action that should be taken when an attempt to connect in error-control mode fails.

0	Attempts V.42 connection. Hangs up if remote modem doesn't support V.42.
3	Makes asynchronous connection. No error control. Same as AT&Q0.
4	Attempts V.42 connection. If attempt fails, attempts MNP 2–4 connection. If attempt fails, then hangs up.
5	Attempts V.42 connection. If attempt fails, attempts MNP 2–4 connection. If attempt fails, then attempts asynchronous connection. (default)

No:	Description	Default	Range
S37	Desired DCE connection speed	0	0/3:11

This value is used in conjunction with the ATN and ATB values to determine which modulations are attempted when connecting.

0	Auto-mode Attempts to connect at the highest possible speed. (default)
3	Attempts to connect at 300 bps.
5	Attempts to connect at 1200 bps.
6	Attempts to connect at 2400 bps.
7	Attempts to connect at 4800 bps.
8	Attempts to connect at 7200 bps.
9	Attempts to connect at 9600 bps.
10	Attempts to connect at 12000 bps.
11	Attempts to connect at 14400 bps.

No:	Description	Default	Range
S38	Delay before hang up(s).	0	0:254
S46	V.42 bis data compression	138	136/138
136	V.42 only		
138	V.42 with V.42 bis compression. (default)		
S48	Feature negotiation action	7	0/3/7/128

Selects which error control features are allowed when making connections.

0	Negotiation disabled: try only V.42.
3	Negotiation enabled without detection phase.
7	Negotiation enabled with detection phase. (default)
128	Negotiation disabled: try MNP only. V.42 disabled.

No:	Description	Default	Range
S95	Error control negotiation message	32	4/8/32

MNP-specific AT commands

AT\Bn Send break Send a break on the line for n times 100 milliseconds (n ranges from 1 to 9).

AT%Cn

Compression enable Enables/disables MNPClass 5 data compression during MNP reliable connections.

0	Disables data compression.
1	Enables MNP 5 data compression. (default)

AT\Gn DCE flow control Enables/disables modem-to-modem flow control. Coupled with \X, which determines if flow control characters are passed through or filtered.

0	Disables modem-to-modem flow control. (default)
1	Enables modem-to-modem flow control.

AT\Nn Selects MNP features.

0-1	Normal mode MNPdisabled.
2	If the remote modem does not support MNP, the local modem hangs up. This is known as the reliable mode.
3	If the remote modem supports MNP, a reliable connection is established. If the remote modem does not support MNP, a normal connection is established. (default). This is known as the auto-reliable mode.

AT\O Treated as ATO0 command. Modem returns to on-line state. MNP Link is not negotiated.

AT\Tn Sets the number of minutes the modem waits before automatically hanging up when data is not sent or received. The default option is disabled.

ATU Treated as ATO0 command. Modem returns to on-line state. MNP link is not terminated.

AT\Vn MNP result code

  0   Disables modified MNP result codes. (default)

  1   Enables modified standard MNP result codes 24 to 28.

  2   Returns OK; no effect.

AT\Xn Flow control processing

  0   No pass-through flow control.

  1   Pass-through flow control.

AT\Y Treated as ATO0 command. Modem returns to on-line state. MNP link is not negotiated.

AT\Z Treated as ATO0 command. Modem returns to on-line state. MNP link is not negotiated.

B How do I do that with Windows NT 3.x

This appendix is a list of instructions for Windows NT v3.x systems based on the common activities and operations defined in Chapter 10. Versions of Windows NT prior to version 4 had slighly different commands and utilities. While it is relatively straightforward to work out how to use or set up an older version, this appendix has been included to make life a little easier. As with chapter 10, there are several methods in some cases.

Changing the system

Changing the desktop

- To change the colours used in the desktop, open the **Color** control panel.

- To change the background and so on, use the **Desktop** control panel.

Changing the video

- To change the size and colour resolution of the video e.g. to move from 640 by 480 to 800 by 600, open the **Display** control panel.

Changing the environmental variables

- Open the **System** control panel. The environmental variables are displayed in the bottom two boxes and can then be modified.

Changing the boot up procedure

- Open the **System** control panel. The names and time out period used during system boot are shown at the top of the window and can be modified.

Changing the date and time formats

- Open the **Date/Time** control panel.

Changing the keyboard layout

- Open the **Windows NT Setup** utility in the Main program group and use the **Options\\Change Mouse or Keyboard** command.

Changing the mouse settings

- To install a different mouse, open the **Windows NT Setup** utility in the Main program group and use the **Options\\Change Mouse or Keyboard** command.

- To change the current mouse settings e.g. speed, resolution and so on, open the **Mouse** control panel.

Changing the sound settings

- Open the **Sound** control panel to assign different sounds to system beeps and so on.

Changing the disk configurations

- Open the **Disk Administrator** utility in the Administrator Tools program.

Adding/removing tape drives

- If a new controller has been added to support the drive, the controller must be installed first. Open the **Windows NT Setup** utility in the Main program group and use the **Options\\Add\Remove Tape controllers** command.

Adding/removing SCSI drives and CD-ROMs

- If a new drive controller has been added to support the drive, the controller must be installed first. Open the **Windows NT Setup** utility in the Main program group and use **the Options\\Add\Remove SCSI controllers** command. After this installation, open the **Disk Administartor** utility in the Administrator Tools program group, partition the disk — **Partition\\Create** — and then format it using **Tools\\Format**.

- If a new CD-ROM controller has been added to support the drive, the controller must be installed first. Open the **Windows NT Setup** utility in the Main program group and use the **Options\\Add\Remove SCSI controllers** command.

Files and directories

Copying

- Open the **File Manager**, select the files and drag them to their destination drive or directory icon.

- Open the **File Manager**, select the files use the **File\\Copy** command.

- Open the **MS-DOS** prompt and use the **Copy** command.

Deleting

- Open the **File Manager**, select the files and press the DEL key.

- Open the **File Manager**, select the files use the **File\\Delete** command.

- Open the **MS-DOS** prompt and use the **Delete** command.

Renaming

- Open the **File Manager**, select the files use the **File\\Rename** command.

- Open the **MS-DOS** prompt and use the **Rename** command.

Moving

- Open the **File Manager**, hold down the ALT key while selecting the files and drag them to their destination drive or directory icon.

- Open the **File Manager**, select the files use the **File\\Move** command.

Backing up

- For small files, open the **File Manager** and copy the files to another disk drive or floppy disk.

- For large files and complete disks, use the **Backup** utility in the Administrative Tools program group.

- To make a copy of a disk, open the **File Manager**, select the disk to be copied from the drive bar and then use the **Disk\\Copy** command.

Finding

- Open the **File Manager**, use the **File\\Search** command.

- Use the **MS-DOS** prompt and the **Dir** command.

Adding more disk space

- To add more space to an existing disk drive, open the **Disk Administrator** utility in the Administrator Tools program group select the drive that needs to be expanded and use the **Partition\\Extend Volume Set** command. If this is dimmed out, extending the size of the drive is not possible.

- If an additional drive has been added to the existing disk controller, open the **Disk Administrator** utility in the Administrator Tools program group, partition the disk — **Partition\\Create** — and then format it using **Tools\\Format**.

- If a new controller has been added to support the drive, the controller must be installed first. Open the **Windows NT Setup** utility in the Main program group and use the **Options\\Add\Remove SCSI controllers** command. After this installation, open the **Disk Administrator** utility in the Administrator Tools program

group, partition the disk — **Partition\\Create** — and
then format it using **Tools\\Format**.

Keyboard alternatives

Moving to different buttons

- Pressing the TAB key will move the highlight to the next
  item e.g. the next button in a dialogue box, the next
  program group in Program Manager and so on.

Using the keyboard instead of a mouse

- Pressing the ALT key will activate the menu bar. Press
  the underlined letter in the required menu name and the
  pull down menu will drop down. The command can be
  selected by using the cursor keys to move the highlight
  or by pressing the underlined letter in the required
  command name. Pressing TAB with a menu pulled
  down, will close the current menu and open the next one.

- Pressing the ENTER key has the same action as clicking
  on the currently selected button or icon.

Navigating the screen

Selecting other applications

- Hold down the ALT key and press the TAB key. A small
  window will appear with the name of the next task or
  application in the task list. If the ALT key is released, that
  task is brought to the foreground. If the TAB key is
  released and pressed again, the next task is displayed and
  so on.

- If the window or just a part of a window of the required
  task or application is visible, just click on it.

- Press the CNTRL and ESC keys together to display a task
  list. Select the required task list and click the Switch To
  button or simply double click the task.

- Pressing the CNTRL, ALT and DEL keys
  simultanaeously will present a dialogue box where one
  of the options is to present the task list. With the task list,
  the task or application can be selected as previously
  described.

Deleting other tasks

- Close the task window. This will exit the task and delete
  it from the current task list.

- Use the Exit command which is typically the last command in the first pull down menu.

- Press the CNTRL and ESC keys together to display a task list. Select the required task list and click the End Task button.

- Pressing the CNTRL, ALT and DEL keys simultanaeously will present a dialogue box where one of the options is to present the task list. With the task list, the task or application can be selected as previously described.

Minimise and maximise windows

- The first method uses the up and down buttons on the top right of the window.

Close window

Minimise window

Maximise window

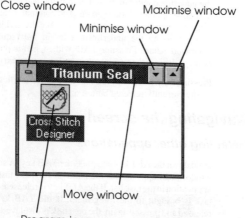

Program icon

Move window

- The second method uses the Minimise and Maximise commands from the window pull down menu as shown.

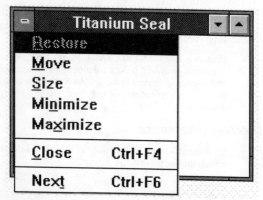

Adjusting windows

- Place the cursor over the edge of the window, hold the mouse button down, wait for it to change to the double headed arrow cursor and move the mouse. The window will change size as required.

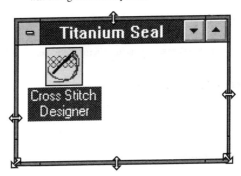

⇕ Change window height

⇔ Change window width

⬿ Change window size

- The second method uses the Size command from the window pull down menu as shown.

Creating a program group

- Go to the Program Manager and use the File\\New command. Select the Program Group option from the resulting dialogue box.

Creating a program item

- Goto the Program Manager and use the File\\New command. Select the Program Item option from the resulting dialogue box. The Common option will create an item that all the users can see.

Deleting a program group

- Select the program group by clicking on it and use the **File\\Delete** command. Alternatively, press the DEL key when the group has been selected.

Deleting a program item

- Select the program item by clicking on it and use the **File\\Delete** command. Alternatively, press the DEL key when the group has been selected.

Networks

Connecting to a network drive

- Open the **File Manager** and use the **Disk\\Connect Network Drive** command.

Disconnecting a network drive

- Open the **File Manager** and use the **Disk\\Disconnect Network Drive** command.

Connecting to a network printer

- Open the **Print Manager** and use the **Printer\\Connect to Printer** command.

Disconnecting a network printer

- Open the **Print Manager** and use the **Printer\\Remove Printer** command.

Adding/removing network boards and drivers

- Use the **Network** control panel.

Passwords

Changing

- Open the **User Manager** utility in the Administrative Tools program group, and double click on the user that needs the password to be changed. The **User Properties** box will appear and the password can be changed.

Forgotten

- Open the **User Manager** utility in the Administrative Tools program group, and double click on the user that needs the password to be changed. The **User Properties** box will appear and the password can be changed. Inform the user of the new password.

Locked out accounts

- Open the **User Manager** utility in the Administrative Tools program group, and double click on the user that needs the password to be changed. The **User Properties** box will appear and the account unlocked by unchecking the **Account Locked Out** box.

Screen savers

- Open the **Desktop** control panel. This allows the screen saver to be enabled and if needed password protected.

Printing

Creating a printer

- Open the **Print Manager** and use the **Printer\\Create Printer** command.

Accessing a printer on another system

- Open the **Print Manager** and use the **Printer\\Connect to Printer** command.

Assigning the default printer

- Open the **Print Manager** and select the printer from the pull down list marked default in the upper right of the window.

Using a different printer

- Open the **Print Manager** and change the default printer.

- Most applications have the ability in the **Print** or **Print Setup** commands to select a different printer.

Deleting documents

- Open the **Print Manager**, double click on a printer icon to display the printer window and its print queue. Select a document and then use the **Document\\Remove Document** command. Alternatively press the DEL key once the document has been selected.

Pausing a printer

- Open the **Print Manager** and use the **Printer\\Pause** command.

Resuming a paused printer

- Open the **Print Manager** and use the **Printer\\Resume** command.

Pausing a document

- Open the **Print Manager**, double click on a printer icon to display the printer window and its print queue. Select a document and then use the **Document\\Pause** command.

Resuming a document

- Open the **Print Manager**, double click on a printer icon to display the printer window and its print queue. Select a document and then use the **Document\\Resume** command.

Setting up the printer

- Open the **Print Manager** and use the **Printer\\Properties** command.

Page sizes

- Open the **Print Manager** and use the **Printer\\Forms** command.

Screen dumps

- To copy the whole screen to the Clipboard, where it can be pasted into a document, press the **Print Screen** key.

- To copy the current window — not the whole screen — to the Clipboard, where it can be pasted into a document, press the **Alt** and **Print Screen** keys together.

- When pasting screen dumps into a Word or Powerpoint document, the image will be automatically scaled to fit the paper size.

INDEX

\# character   156
£ character   156
32 bit addressing   14–18
32 bit processing   14–18
6502   1
80x86   2, 18, 25, 212

A

Accessibility options   141–143
Accessing a printer on another system   245
Accessories   59–102
Accessories window group   59
Accounts   206, 244
Add/remove Program Properties   143–145
Adding more disk space   240
Adding/removing network boards   244
Adjusting windows   242
Administration tools   30, 56, 140
Administrative Tools   201, 240, 244
Administrative tools   201
Administrator   2, 17, 29, 112, 127, 148, 161, 201, 205, 206, 207-210, 212, 213, 218, 223, 239–241
Administrator Tools   239, 240, 241
Apple   1, 30, 36, 54, 111, 136, 137, 139, 169, 184, 199, 230
Apple MAC   30, 36, 54, 184
Apple Mac   1, 137
Apple Macintosh   1, 101
AppleTalk   111, 136, 137, 139, 183, 189, 199, 230
AppleTalk printer   183–185
ASCII setup   81
Assigning the defulat printer   245
AT command strings   80
ATAPI CD-ROM   26
Audit   2, 19, 206, 208, 216

B

Background   6, 10, 20, 28, 68, 69, 162, 168, 169, 180, 199, 238
Backup   223–228
Baud rate_   77
Bindings   126
Bindings sub-panel   126
BIOS ROM   22
Booting Windows NT   26–28

C

C language   1, 18, 29, 210, 226
Calculator   59–60
Cardfile   61–64
CD   88, 90, 91, 92
CD Player   90–91
CD-ROM   21, 22, 25, 26, 29, 88, 90, 91, 123, 157, 177, 233, 239
Changing the
    Boot up procedure   238
    CD-ROM drives   239
    Date and time formats   238
    Desktop   238
    Disk configurations   239
    Environmental variables   238
    Keyboard layout   238

Mouse settings 238
SCSI drives 239
Sound settings 239
Tape drives 239
Video 238
Changing the system 238–239
Character map 89–90
Chat 70
Clipboard 43, 60, 62, 65, 67, 83, 87, 90, 92, 94, 105, 195, 196, 246
Clipbook viewer 101
Clock 60–61
COM1 76, 149
COM2 150, 182
COM3 80, 149
COM4 80, 150
Common window menus 42–47
communications protocol 76
CompuServe 30
Computers 111–113
Configuring a printer 188–194
Connecting to a network drive 244
Connecting to a network printer 244
Connecting to an AppleTalk printer 183–185
Connecting to network disk drives 127–128
Console Window Properties 145, 145–147
Context switch 4, 5, 7, 8
Control Panel 30,32, 38, 42, 52, 57
Desktop 153–155
Devices 173
Fonts 147
Keyboard 153–155
Network settings 172
Ports 148–150
Services 173
Sound 172
Sound Mapper 172
UPS 173
CONTROL-ALT-DELETE 19, 34, 42, 160, 169
Controlling a printer 194–198
Controlling a printer queue 198–200
Creating a printer 245
Creating a program group 243
Cursor blink rate 153
Cursors 151
Cut 3, 4, 6, 8, 11, 12, 17, 24, 32, 35–38, 43, 48, 62, 65, 67, 69,
     77, 92, 94, 104–105, 150, 195, 203, 206, 212

D

Date and Time 166–167
David Cutler 3
DEC 3
DEC Alpha 25
Deleting a program group 243
Deleting a program item 243
Deleting documents 245
Deleting other tasks 242
Desktop 8, 26, 30–32, 37, 52, 53, 57, 66, 68, 153, 168, 238
Disconnecting a network drive 244
Disconnecting a network printer 244
Disk Administrator 209, 209–216, 210, 212, 213, 239, 240, 241
Disk drive 23, 48, 54, 55, 56, 111, 122, 127, 210, 233, 240
Disk format 213–237
Disk label 214
Disk partition 210–213
Display 232

Display settings 167–171
DMA channels 22
Document control 194–198
Document Defaults 199
Documents 199–200
Domains 111–113
Dragging 32, 35, 37, 48, 49, 52, 70, 225
Drive Information 233
Drive Letter 214

E

EIA-232_ 76
Environment 235
Ethernet 114
Event 4, 6, 7, 8, 10, 27, 29, 161, 208, 216, 217, 218, 219, 230, 237
Event Viewer 208, 216
Event viewer 29
Explore facility 54
Explorer 30, 37–42, 103–110, 127, 180
    ToolBar 109–110
    Window 103–104

F

FAT 17, 22, 23, 29, 111, 132, 209, 210, 211, 212
File Manager 30, 37, 49, 52–56, 103, 123, 209, 213, 224, 225
File manager 224
File system 10, 17–23, 28, 40–43, 48, 52, 53, 56, 103, 105, 200, 209–214, 225, 233
File system icons 103
Files and directories 239–241
    Backing up 240
    Copying 239
    Deleting 239
    Finding 240
    Moving 240
    Renaming 240
Floppy disk 21, 22, 25, 26, 29, 122, 160, 212, 213, 223
Fonts 147–148
Fonts control panel 147–148
Foreground 6, 10, 20, 162, 222, 241
FTP 30, 116, 124, 172
Ftp.microsoft.com 30

G

Group Membership 203

H

HAL 10, 18
Hard disk 24, 29, 113, 157, 233
Hardware profiles 162
Hayes (AT) command strings 80
Headphone socket 88
HPFS 17, 23
HyperTerminal 70–86, 148, 163, 164, 183

I

I/O address 120, 121
IBM 10, 82, 90, 137
IDE 26
IDE drivers 26

Imaging   101
installation commands   24–25
Installation procedure   21–24, 25–26
Installing a printer   182–187
Installing multiple printers   187
Installing network support   113–118
Intel   2, 3, 18, 25, 29, 123
Internet control panel   150
Interrupt   4, 7, 8, 10, 11, 12, 18, 22, 80, 120–122, 149–150
Interrupt level   10, 18, 22, 80, 120, 121, 122, 150

K

Kernel   4, 5, 7, 8, 12, 15, 16, 17, 18
Kernel mode   12, 15, 16
Keyboard
    Auto repeat   153
Keyboard alternatives   241
    Moving to different buttons   241
    Using the keyboard instead of a mouse   241

L

LAN Manager   3, 111, 116, 124
Lana number   125
Left mouse button   35
Local Group   204
Locked out accounts   244
Logical drive   127, 210, 211
Logoff   42, 43, 104, 194
Logon   19, 29, 99, 128, 203
LPC   16, 17
LPT1   182

M

M68000   1
Making disks shareable   129–135
Maximise   30, 32, 33, 34
Media player   91–92
Memory   2, 4, 11, 12, 14, 15, 16, 19, 24, 28, 29, 158, 161, 162, 194, 230
Memory manager   16
Microsoft Internet site   30
MIDI   92, 177
MIDI Mapper   174
Minimise   16, 30, 31, 32, 33, 34, 242
MIPS   25
Modem_   73, 76
Mouse   150, 151, 151–153, 153, 170, 211, 212, 225, 238, 241, 243
MS-DOS   1–6, 11, 12–22, 25–
            27, 39, 111, 132, 145, 158, 160, 203, 209, 210, 223, 239, 240
Multi-tasking   4, 5, 6, 9, 11, 18, 180
Multi-threaded   2, 12, 13, 17
Multimedia   174, 174–179
Multiple permissions   136
Multiple shares   135
Multiple threads   12, 17
Multitasking   1, 3–11
My Computer   30, 42, 48, 52–56, 58, 127, 180

N

NetBIOS   125
NetBUEI   116, 124
Netware   3, 116, 124

Network   235
   AppleTalk support   136–139
   Bindings   117
   Hardware installation   113
   Software installation   113–119
network card   114
Network Drive   128, 129, 244
Network drive   127, 128, 129, 131, 134, 203, 244
Network Neighborhood   42, 48, 56, 57, 127
Network Neighbourhood   30
Network printer   244
Network settings   172
Network support   113–118
Network wizard   113
Notepad   64–65
Novell   116, 124
Nstallation variations   29
NTFS   17, 209, 211
Numeric keypad   151
NW Link IPX/SPX   116, 124

O

Object Packager   101
OS/2   15, 17, 23

P

Page sizes   246
Paintbrush   66–70
Panasonic   26
Panasonic CD-ROM   26
Paper size   199
Password   26, 128, 201–207, 244, 245
Passwords
   Changing   244
   Forgotten   244
Paste   43, 59, 60, 62, 65, 67, 68, 83, 87, 94, 105, 196
Pausing a document   246
Pausing a printer   245
Pel   69
Performance Monitor   219, 219–223, 220, 222
Permissions   112, 131, 132, 134, 135
Phone Dialler   100
Pixel elements   69
Pointers   151
Portability   1
POSIX   2
PostScript   148, 189
PowerPC   2, 25
Print Manager   180, 181, 198, 199
Print manager   29, 148
Print queue control   194–198
Print server   29
Print spooler   230
Printer   3, 26, 29, 62, 76, 83, 111, 113, 127, 136, 137, 148, 156, 171,
    172, 180, 184, 189, 193, 194, 198, 199, 218, 244, 245, 246
   Properties   199
Printer configuration   188–194
Printer control   194–198
Printer installation   182–187
   Multiple printers   187
Printer queue control   198–200
Printer wizard   182
Printer\\Properties   246
Printers control panel   38, 156, 180–181, 182

Printing   180–200
    AppleTalk printer   183–185
Priority   4–13, 16, 17, 20, 175, 177, 189, 199
Priority level   4, 9, 10, 11, 16, 189
Prism project   3
ProComm   4
Program crash   19
Program group   23, 29, 30, 33, 37, 43, 90, 104, 140, 194, 201, 223,
        238, 239, 240, 241, 243, 244, 245
Program item   103, 243
Program Manager   30, 31, 37, 43, 54, 103, 104, 123
Programs sub-menu.   23
Properties   57
Protection   11, 12, 19, 160
Protocols sub-panel   123–124
PSOS   9

R

'Ready' list   4
Real time   6–11, 16
Recovery   19, 21, 26, 27, 28, 158, 160
Regional control panel   156–157
Registry   140
Remote Access Admin   236–237
Reset   160, 199, 206, 211
Resources   234
Resuming a document   246
Resuming a paused printer   246
Right mouse button   35
RS-232   76

S

Scanners   101
Scrapbook   101
Screen colour resolution   170
Screen dumps   246
Screen savers   245
screen size   170
SCSI   22, 26, 223, 230, 239, 241
SCSI Adapters   157–158
Security   2, 15, 17, 18, 22, 26, 201, 206–208, 216, 217
Selecting other applications   241
Semaphore   17
Serial port_   76, 77
Server   29, 56, 111, 112, 113, 129, 171
Service List   230
Services   173
Services sub-panel   125
Setting up the printer   246
Settings\\Taskbar   23
Sharing   1, 4, 54, 127, 130, 135, 149, 150, 171
Shutdown   19, 41, 42, 43, 104, 148, 180
Sound   172
Sound Mapper   174
Sound recorder   87–88
SoundBlaster   22, 26, 90, 92, 175, 177
Start bit_   77
Start button   23, 37, 140, 180, 243
Status bar   44, 90, 103,106, 196, 200, 215, 222, 227
Stop bit_   77
Synchronisation   17
System   158–162, 229
System check   28–29
SYSTEM.INI   140

T

Tape Devices 165–166
Tape drive installation 223–224
TAPI 30, 71, 72, 163, 164
Task 1–11, 18–20, 123, 162, 168, 180, 181, 241, 242
Task list 31, 34, 241, 242
Taskbar 31, 32, 34, 34–35, 35, 38, 49, 51, 103, 140, 145,
    options 51
Tasking 162
TCP/IP 3, 99, 116, 124
Telephony 163–165
Telnet 99, 99–102
Terminal 70, 71, 72
Terminal Configuration 82
Terminate and stay resident 4
Time slice 4
Title bar 61, 228
Token Ring 114
Toolbar 34, 38, 44, 49, 53, 90, 106, 196, 222, 227
Truetype 148
TSR. *See* Terminate and stay resident

U

UART 77
uninterruptible power supply 173
Universal asynchronous receiver transmitter 77
UNIX 1, 3, 4, 5, 28, 116, 124
UPS 173
User Environment Profile 204
User Manager 201–209
    New User 202
    Policies 206–208
    Properties 205
User profiles 162
User rights 207
Using a different printer 245

V

Version 228
VGA 170
Video for Windows 92, 175
Virtual memory 14, 15, 16, 158, 161
VMS 1, 3, 5
Volume accessory 177
Volume control 88
Volume Set 211
VT100 terminal 82

W

Wang 101
WFW3.11 networking 113
Wild card 39
Wild card characters 39
WIN16 14, 20
WIN32 14, 15, 16, 17
Windows 3.1 1–6, 9–23, 26, 59, 80, 87, 140, 141, 149–
    151, 160, 161, 167, 168, 172, 175, 177, 203, 223
Windows 3.1 shell 30, 42
Windows '95 1, 3, 9, 21–24, 30, 31, 35, 116, 124, 129
Windows '95 desktop 31–34

Windows '95 networking   113
Windows '95 shell   30–58
    Control Panel   42
    Copying and moving files   35
    Documents menu   38
    Edit menu   43–44, 105–106
    Explore command   48–49
    File menu   43, 104–105
    Find\\All Files   39–40
    Find\\Computer   41
    Help menu   47, 109, 198, 200
    My computer   52–56
    Network Neighborhood   56–57
    Properties   54–56
    Recycle Bin   36–37
    Right hand button tricks   57–58
    Run   41
    Settings options   38
    Shortcuts   36
    Shutdown   41
    Start Menu Programs   49
    Taskbar configuration   49
    Taskbar options   51
    Tools menu   48–49
    View menu   44–47, 106–109
    Window handling   32–33
    Window menu   33–34
    Windows NT Explorer   37–42
Windows for Workgroups   1, 3, 111, 116, 124, 129
Windows Help system   47, 109, 198, 200
Windows NT
    characteristics   9
    I/O support   18
    Interrupt priorities   10–11
    Networking support   2
    Portability   1
    Process priorities   9–10
Windows NT Diagnostics   228–236
Windows NT Explorer   42
Windows NT help   64, 88, 91, 92, 99
Windows NT logo   28
Windows NT networking   113
Winnt command 21, 24, 25
    Options   24–25
Winnt32   24, 25
wizard   114
WordPad   93–96
WordStar   4
Workgroups   111–113
Workstation   1, 3, 22, 25, 27, 29, 56, 70, 111, 113, 129, 137

Z

Z80   1